Observations of a
Bahai Traveller

Also from Westphalia Press
westphaliapress.org

The Idea of the Digital University

Bulwarks Against Poverty in America

Treasures of London

Avate Garde Politician

L'Enfant and the Freemasons

Baronial Bedrooms

Making Trouble for Muslims

Philippine Masonic Directory ~ 1918

Paddle Your Own Canoe

Opportunity and Horatio Alger

Careers in the Face of Challenge

Bookplates of the Kings

The Boy Chums Cruising in Florida Waters

Freemasonry in Old Buffalo

Original Cables from the Pearl Harbor Attack

Social Satire and the Modern Novel

The Essence of Harvard

The Genius of Freemasonry

A Definitive Commentary on Bookplates

James Martineau and Rebuilding Theology

No Bird Lacks Feathers

Gems of Song for the Eastern Star

Crime 3.0

Anti-Masonry and the Murder of Morgan

Understanding Art

Spies I Knew

Lodge "Himalayan Brotherhood" No. 459 C.E.

Ancient Masonic Mysteries

Collecting Old Books

Masonic Secret Signs and Passwords

Death Valley in '49

Lariats and Lassos

Mr. Garfield of Ohio

The Wisdom of Thomas Starr King

The French Foreign Legion

War in Syria

Naturism Comes to the United States

New Sources on Women and Freemasonry

Designing, Adapting, Strategizing in Online Education

Gunboat and Gun-runner

Meeting Minutes of Naval Lodge No. 4 F.A.A.M ~ 1812 & 1813

Observations of a Bahai Traveller

by Charles Mason Remey

WESTPHALIA PRESS
An imprint of Policy Studies Organization

Observations of a Bahai Traveller
All Rights Reserved © 2014 by Policy Studies Organization

Westphalia Press
An imprint of Policy Studies Organization
1527 New Hampshire Ave., NW
Washington, D.C. 20036
info@ipsonet.org

ISBN-13: 978-1633910515
ISBN-10: 1633910512

Cover design by Taillefer Long at Illuminated Stories:
www.illuminatedstories.com

Daniel Gutierrez-Sandoval, Executive Director
PSO and Westphalia Press

Devin Proctor, Director of Media and Publications
PSO and Westphalia Press

Updated material and comments on this edition
can be found at the Westphalia Press website:
www.westphaliapress.org

OBSERVATIONS
OF A
BAHAI TRAVELLER
1908

BY

CHARLES MASON REMEY

SECOND EDITION
PUBLISHED
November,
1914

ABDUL—BAHA

PREFACE.

Acting upon the suggestion of Abdul-Baha, I wrote this account of travels made among some Bahais of the Orient during the summer of 1908, the first edition of which was published in pamphlet form the year following my tour.

Last month I again had the blessing of a visit with Abdul-Baha who was then upon Mount Carmel in Syria. While with him I sought his counsel regarding the advisability of this second edition, the first one having been practically exhausted. He advised republication—hence this volume, the material of which is substantially the same as that of the former edition, save that a brief historical sketch of the founders of the movement has been added for the benefit of those who may not be familiar with the cause.

Through this narrative of travel, I hope to share with the reader some of that faith in things divine, and that spirit of brotherly love which one receives so bounteously through contact with Abdul-Baha and association with those who have been touched by the spirit of the cause which he represents.

C. M. R.,
26 November, 1914.   Washington, D. C.

HISTORICAL SKETCH OF THE FOUNDERS OF THE BAHAI MOVEMENT.

On May 23, 1844, there appeared in Shiraz, Persia, a young man, Ali Mohammed by name, who declared himself to be The Bab,* the forerunner of "Him Whom God would Manifest," a great teacher who was soon to appear with manifest signs of divine power and strength, through whose teachings the divine unity of mankind would be established.

The Bab was immediately met by great opposition on the part of the Mussulman clergy, and at their instigation was placed under military surveillance. In spite of being thus hampered He continued teaching, exhorting the people to holiness and sanctity of living, in order that they might be fitted to meet the Promised One, shortly to appear, and to become as mirrors reflecting His spiritual perfection.

Thus the first two years of The Bab's ministry passed, at the end of which time He was seized, by the order of the clerical authorities, and thrust into prison. His imprisonment lasted four

---
*The Arabic word for door or gate.

years, during which time He taught His followers through letters and epistles. This was followed by a trial in which The Bab was condemned to death upon the charge of heresy. He, with one of His followers, suffered martyrdom in the cause of truth in the city of Tabriz, Persia, on July 9, 1851.

The mission of The Bab being that of precursor of "Him Whom God would Manifest," the institutions and ordinances which He established were for the time being only. With the appearance of the Promised One, His followers (the Babis), were commanded to turn their faces unto Him, when He, who was to come, would establish His cause which would bring spiritual peace and harmony upon earth.

The Bab was not alone in being persecuted by the Mohammedans; with His martyrdom came upon His followers troubles of the most dire nature. Over twenty thousands of these willingly gave up their property, families, and lives, rather than deny and recant their faith. These persecutions are by no means a thing of the past, for in Persia, as late as 1901, there were one hundred and seventy-nine martyrs at one time in the cities of Yazd and Esphahan.

A BAHAI TRAVELLER

During the days of The Bab's ministry, while His cause was being promulgated by His followers throughout Persia, there were many believers who never met with Him in person. Among these was Baha'o'llah, a young man of noble family, who warmly espoused The Bab's cause, publicly upholding and teaching it in Teheran.

In 1852, the year following The Bab's martyrdom, when the persecution of the Babis was at its height, Baha'o'llah, with others of the new faith, was imprisoned in Teheran, and later on with a number of Babis was sent in exile to Baghdad in Irak.

During the exile in Baghdad, Baha'o'llah, through His teachings and spiritual insight, gradually brought calmness and assurance to the followers. As the movement gained strength the local clerical authorities began to fear His influence. This led to an arrangement made by which Baha'o'llah, with the band of believers, was ordered to a more distant exile in Constantinople. In April, 1862, on the eve of His departure from Irak, Baha'o'llah declared Himself to a few chosen ones amongst the followers to be The One Whose coming The Bab had foretold, "He Whom God would Manifest."

From Constantinople the exiles were sent to Adrianople, where they remained until 1868, when they were finally sent to the fortified town of Akka (Acre), a penal colony on the Mediterranean just north of Mt. Carmel in Syria.

Here in the land of Carmel, where "the coming," in this latter day has been foretold, Baha'o'llah lived and taught; many traveled from great distances to receive instructions from Him, while others received teaching through His writings.

Thus it will be seen that with the coming of Baha'o'llah, the mission and teachings of The Bab were fulfilled and completed, so from that time on the movement became known as the Bahai Movement, and the believers became known as Bahais. In the Spring of 1892, the mission of Baha'o'llah being finished, He passed quietly from this world. During His ministry His cause was not explained nor established in the world in general. To this end Baha'o'llah, in His testament, as well as in various parts of His teachings, commanded His followers upon His departure to turn their faces toward His eldest son, Abdul-Baha, whom He had chosen as their spiritual guide—"The Center of His Covenant" to the people of the world, the expounder of His teachings, the one who would establish His cause in the world, the one upon whose shoulders His mantle would fall.

Abdul-Baha was born in Teheran, in Persia, on the 23d day of May, 1844, the day upon which The Bab began His teaching. During all the trials and vicissitudes of the mission of Baha'o'llah, His son, Abdul-Baha, was at His right hand promulgating His cause and serving His followers. He was the first of all to recognize Baha'o'llah as The Promised One; accordingly from childhood Abdul-Baha was destined to become the center of the movement.

ABDUL-BAHA makes but one claim for himself as to his spiritual station, that of SERVICE in the path of God. He signs himself, "Abdul-Baha Abbas," which being translated is "Abbas, the Servant of God." Abdul-Baha is acknowledged by all of the Bahais as their spiritual leader, and the one to be emulated in the teaching of this great faith in the world. He, through his example and service to humanity, is bringing the spiritual life of Baha'o'llah within the reach of the Bahais. He is the first fruit of the cause of Baha'o'llah in the world, and he is the center from which the light of interpretation of the Bahai Cause is now being radiated to all the people of the world; therefore, he, in his mission, lives and exemplifies his title of "The Center of The Covenant."

INTRODUCTION.

Asia, the continent from which the Caucasian peoples swept westward to rule the world, has in like manner been the land from whence has come spiritual sustenance for mankind—his religion. In her mountains, the prophets communed with God and revealed His life-giving Word; and from her shores their followers embarked to carry the messages of truth to the nations of the West.

Civilization is the outward expression of the inner or spiritual condition of a people. The civilization of the West is in reality the fruit of the religion, which it has received from the East. The Orient is the mother, who has sent forth a man child, which is the Occident. Now that mother has grown old. She has been plundered and pillaged by her offspring of the West, and is helpless. The time is at hand for the Occident to go to her help, and in the spirit of love serve her and lift her from her present condition. By so doing the West will gain abundantly—gain through giving as well as receiving, for the Orient has much to give to the West.

As with woman, the strength of the Orient

manifests itself through those soul characteristics that are subjective rather than objective; while, on the other hand, as with man, the strength of the Occident manifests itself through those soul characteristics that are objective rather than subjective.

The man who seeks the masculine virtues in woman is quite as sure to be disappointed as is the Occidental who visits the Orient with the expectation of there finding people fashioned after the standard of the West. The wise man seeks in woman those feminine virtues wherein she is strong and, by union with her, finds a balance which his masculine nature needs. In this manner is it not necessary that the Occident and Orient should come together? Where the one is strong, the other is weak; and where the one is weak, the other is strong. Through this unity the highest and most noble in each is forthcoming.

Until the present time the western nations that have gone into the Orient have gone to conquer. They have succeeded in subjugating the people, but they have not won them. They have always remained strangers in a strang land. There has been no union between them and the Oriental peoples and, consequently, but little lasting good has come to either from their meeting.

Woman may be subjugated by man, but, unless she is won by love, this subjugation narrows her character and life and tends to develop everything save her better and nobler nature. This is the condition of the Orient of to-day. While her people have a certain respect for the superior power of the West, nevertheless a great chasm separates the two—an abyss which can be bridged only through awakening in each a love for the other. As man's love-union with woman marks an epoch in the development of his character and opens before him a field of hitherto unknown possibilities, so the uniting of the Occident with the Orient will be productive of the greatest good to the world.

Again in these latter days another spiritual message is coming to the world from the Orient through the Bahai Movement, the rise and early growth of which in many respects resembles that of primitive Christianity.

The object of this movement is the religious unity of all peoples. It offers to the world a spiritual teaching which builds upon the teachings of the religions of the past and present, fulfilling their hopes and prophecies, and uniting all peoples, both East and West, in the spirit of God's Kingdom upon earth.

This cause has come into the world in order to establish peace—the oneness of all humanity —through implanting in the hearts of men the true and vital spirit of the religions of the past. It comes to perfect and to fulfil—not to destroy. It confirms one's faith in his own religion and makes him firm in the reality thereof, and it leads him to the realization that all men are his brothers and that the Kingdom of Heaven is now actually with us here upon earth, which is the one great truth and the one great theme of all true religion.

All religions teach the coming of spiritual oneness and harmony on earth, and in the holy books of each are the promises of the coming of a great teacher or Divine Manifestation Who is to appear in the latter days and establish this divine order of things in the world. In this way does the coming of the Bahai teachers fulfil the prophecies of the past, while the spirit of brotherhood and love engendered by this cause is uniting thousands of Christians, Jews, Moslems,

THE DRIVE FROM HAIFA TO AKKA.

Hindus, Buddhists, Zoroastrians and others in the spirit of the oneness of humanity.

This movement had its birth in the East and like the other phases of the one truth, which was revealed by all the prophets, it has worked its way westward until now its adherents encircle the earth. Under its invigorating spiritual power, its followers in the Orient are awakening to and seeking the advantages of western civilization and are helping conditions there by ministering physically, morally and spiritually to the people about them; while in the Occident, the same force is giving people calmness, assurance, and poise of soul, which the strenuousness of western life has all but destroyed.

Under the guidance of its three inspired leaders, The Bab, who was the forerunner and the First Point of this revelation, Baha'o'llah, who was the revealer of The Word, and Abdul-Baha, who is the expounder of The Word, the Bahai Movement is breaking down the barriers between the various religious systems and, through its vital divine power, is uniting all human elements in one great universal brotherhood that is destined to grow and expand until it fills the world. This is that which was foretold by the prophets and seers of the past. It is the establishment of God's Kingdom among men, and it is the nucleus from which will evolve the great universal or world civilization which will become realized as peoples of all the nations, races and religions become spiritually and materially united.

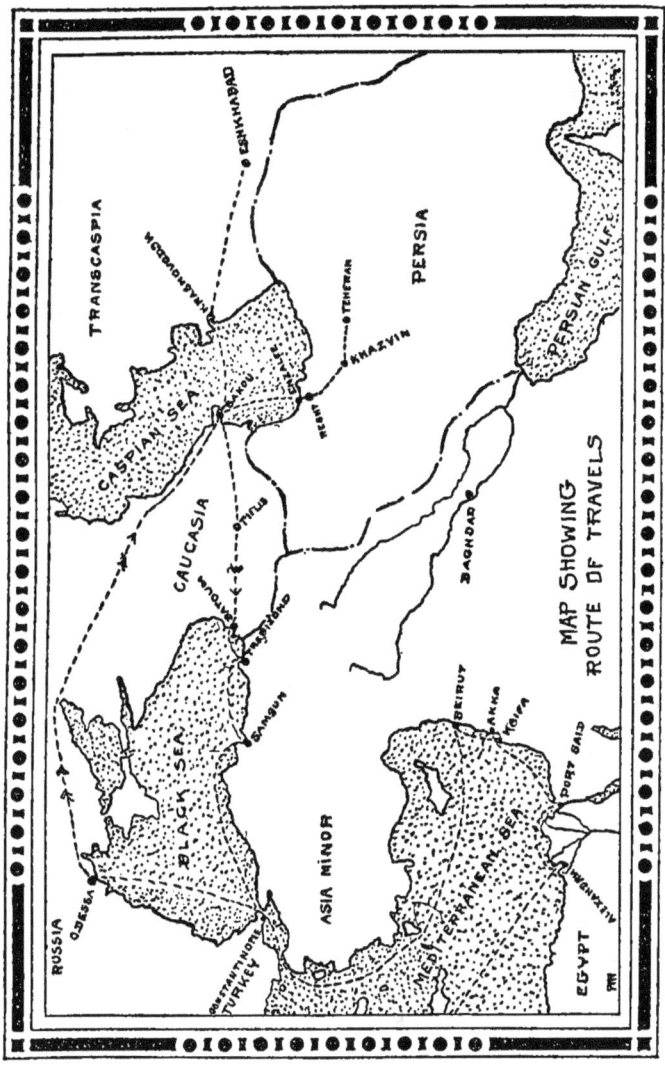

NARRATIVE.

For some time prior to leaving America for the East, in April, 1908, I had been in correspondence with an American friend and co-worker in the Bahai Cause, in the hope that we would be able to arrange to make together a trip into Turkestan and Persia. It was not, however, until our meeting in London early in the following month that our plan of travel was finally mapped out and decided upon.

My friend had, for several years, been engaged in the Bahai work in London and was, at that moment, unable to leave England, so it was arranged that we should meet in Vienna about three weeks later, from whence we planned to travel eastward. His route to Vienna lay through Brussels and Stuttgart, while mine was via Paris, Stuttgart and Munich, which places are all Bahai centers.

I must not omit a paragraph regarding the Bahai work now being carried on in Stuttgart. Eight months previous to the visit of which I write I spent a few days there where then was but a handful of Bahais. This time, however, I found an organized assembly, with many people busily engaged in serving the cause by translating and publishing Bahai literature, as well as by organizing meetings for teaching and study and like work. One very enthusiastic believer was erecting a building in which he was making provision for an assembly room, which, when completed, would be a home and a center for the Bahais. In many ways I saw the firmness with which these friends had grasped the teachings and were working out its principles. During the intervening eight months, Miss Alma Knobloch of Washington had been teaching in Stuttgart, and the fruits of her efforts and those of her friends were easily seen in the work of that assembly. When the organs of the body are all working and performing each its own function, then the body is vigorous and strong. So it is with an assembly of friends in which each is doing its own part. As individuals they do not necessarily attract much attention, yet the power of the assembly as a whole is strongly felt.

On the eve of our planned departure from Vienna, a tablet (letter) was received from Abdul-Baha, which opened the way for me to visit

Akka on my way out to the East. Although I had hoped to be able to make this visit, yet, on account of governmental troubles then rife throughout Turkish domains, I had no anticipation of realizing my desire. Despite the abrupt change in our plans, everything arranged itself quite well. My going to Syria gave my friend a much desired opportunity to visit a brother Bahai in Constantinople. Traveling leisurely by steamer down the Danube and through the Black Sea he reached Constantinople and completed a visit there of three weeks by the time I joined him. In the mean time my route took me the length of Italy, through Greece and down into Egypt before I reached Syria.

I must pause a moment to write of some friends whom I met in Florence, friends who are spiritual seekers and who received me with open arms, although I had only known them through correspondence. Sig. Arturo Reghini, one of the founders, and the leading spirit of the Biblioteca Filosofica, 5 Piazzale Donatello, Florence, had, during the year past, delivered a course of lectures upon the Bahai Movement. These were

THE LAND APPROACH TO THE CITY OF AKKA.

A BAHAI TRAVELLER

attended by thinking people who are awake to the present day spiritual conditions and necessities, and to many of these the Bahai Movement appealed strongly. That which was most noticeable and attractive in this philosophical center was the kindly spirit which the people bore towards all religious movements, and this was truly Bahai in character.

After brief meetings with the Bahais in Alexandria and Port Said, I took steamer from the latter port to Haifa, where I landed after a voyage of twenty-four hours. Many Bahai pilgrims to the Holy Land have described Haifa and Mount Carmel, yet each takes away with him impressions impossible to put into words. This mountain, in which lived the prophet Elijah, and from Old Testament days considered the Lord's own ground, has, during the past half century, again been the center of renewed spiritual activities, the glad tidings of which are now being heralded the world around.

The foreshadowing of this latter-day movement we see in the expectant veneration with which this spot is held by Christians, Jews, and

Moslems. All three reverence its holy places, for in the sacred writings of each are many prophecies regarding the triumphal coming of the Messiah, and of the transformation of this land and her people from sterility and poverty to fertility and power. Here are several religious communities, monasteries and convents, as well as the German Temple Colony situated on the lower slope of the mountain. This latter was founded in the sixties under a religious enthusiasm which had its birth in Würtemberg.

Off to the north of Mount Carmel, across the Bay of Haifa, is the town of Akka. Built on a rock, surrounded on three sides by the sea, the fourth by a moat and the land, she appears to float on the water. From without, her white fortifications, domes, and turrets, beneath a brilliant sun, with their high lights and black shadows, are strikingly symbolic of the spiritual conditions of light and darkness which have existed within those prison walls. Here, for years, under conditions almost too dreadful to be described, was confined the world's great teacher, Baha'o'llah. He, with about seventy followers, storm-tossed exiles, after years of persecution for His faith, was finally brought in captivity to the dungeon of Akka, within whose darkened recesses languished many a political prisoner, thief and murderer.

It is amid the particles of matter, torn by the forces of the elements from the mountain side and carried down into the valley, that seeds find root, grow and bring forth their fruits. In like manner do we see, in the spiritual history of the world, that, amid the ruin brought about by man, spirituality has had its growth and fruition—out of the blackest darkness has come the most brilliant light. This is strikingly brought to one while in Akka. That Akka, the scene of the bloodiest combats of the Crusades and, in more modern times, of the Napoleonic war in Syria, many times leveled to the ground and finally a penal colony under the late despotic government of Turkey—that this should be the place from which should go forth to the world the great spiritual message of peace, uniting men of all nations and races in brotherly love—is, indeed, in accordance with the marvelous workings of God as we view them in the past and present.

During the winter previous to the visit of which I write, it was generally known amongst the Bahais that Abdul-Baha and the friends in Akka were in trouble, while but few, if any, of us in the West realized how serious was the condition there. The cause of this was the general corruption of the old regime of Turkish government, that reached its climax just before the declaration of a constitutional form of government in Constantinople, which took place but a few weeks after my visit of which I now write. The Bahais in and about Akka were exiles in a foreign land and, being without temporal power or protection, were considered as legitimate plunder by certain officials then in power. Abdul-Baha told me that he had received threatening messages from a very high official, temporally over him, to which he had replied, saying that he was Abdul-Baha (the servant of God), that were that official to exalt him, he would still be Abdul-Baha, were he to oppress him he would still be Abdul-Baha, and were he to kill him, yet would his station ever be the same, Abdul-Baha.

During the five days I waited in Haifa, before it was possible to proceed to Akka, the troublous condition was to some extent ameliorated by the liberating from the prison of

A BAHAI TRAVELLER

Akka of four recent converts to the faith, who had, for several months, been confined there because of their allegiance to the cause. About this time a special guard placed before the house of Abdul-Baha to watch its inmates, was by order of the governor removed, so matters began to take on a less troubled aspect.

Notwithstanding these changes for the better, I had to be very careful in entering and leaving the city. Abdul-Baha's house being watched by spies, I did not go there, but spent the two days and two nights of my visit within the confines of the house of Aga Seyed Taghi Afnan, the venerable Bahai under whose direction the arrangements for the building of the Mashrak-El-Azcar in Eshkhabad were made and executed. Here Abdul-Baha came to see me twice each day. Despite the agitated conditions—for his followers had been almost panic-stricken—Abdul-Baha was calm and evidently very happy. The strain of many years of trouble had left its imprint upon the physical man, but his soul, so emancipated, was brimming over with the love and joy of the Lord.

I could not help comparing this visit to Abdul-Baha with the first visit I, together with several believers, had with him, late in the winter of 1901, at which time he was comparatively free from worldly troubles, being allowed by the governor of Akka to reside temporarily in Haifa. Our party of nine American and European pilgrims were in his house. Then the approach of a Bahai was an easy matter: we went about the town mingling freely with people, and meeting them socially as one would have done in any place. But as I recall those days I remember that our leader often looked distressed. Then the cause in the West was not united spiritually as it is now. While many were attracted and the movement was growing, yet the believers were in danger. They were as young trees enveloped by the blast of the winter's gale. This Abdul-Baha knew and realized while we did not, and, notwithstanding his own ease, it weighed upon him. Now all was reversed. He was in trouble, but those over whom he had so diligently watched and prayed had, through his labor and sacrifices, grown strong in spirit and were uniting in serving humanity as he by his example had taught them to do. Now the unity and the steadfastness of the Bahais being accomplished, his own present troubles were as naught.

A BAHAI TRAVELLER

Abdul-Baha spoke at some length regarding the uniting of the people of the West with those of the East—their spiritual unity—which is bringing about the regeneration of mankind. Now we have in the world of man all the elements for the progress of the people save the one necessary element—the element of love by which all must be brought together and assimilated into one. The heart of the world is tired and sick because it needs the balm of the love of God. This is what Baha'o'llah brought into the world—the power of uniting all in one—and this is what Abdul-Baha, by his life and teaching, is exemplifying and literally infusing into souls.

The home of the Afnan* in Akka, where I was entertained, was a house in which Baha'o'llah had lived for some years. Like many Syrian houses, the lower story with its walls several feet in thickness and high, massive, vaulted ceilings, was used for mercantile purposes, while the upper floor, reached from the street by a heavily barred door, court and steep stone staircase, was the dwelling. This house has been purchased by an American Bahai (a lady who has spent much time in Akka), that, on account of its associa-

---
*Afnan is the name applied to the relatives of The Bab.

tions, it may always remain in Bahai hands.

One room, surrounded by loggias overlooking the sea, was that which had been occupied by Baha'o'llah, while a smaller one next to it, formerly occupied by Abdul-Baha, was the one in which I was lodged. This room, measuring perhaps twelve by sixteen feet, with the exception of the ceiling—the woodwork of which was beamed and panelled and painted in various colors—was devoid of ornamentation.. The walls were washed with lime into which had been inserted sufficient blueing to take away the disagreeable glare of a large white wall surface. Its furnishings consisted of a straw matting on the floor, with a divan along one side of the room which was covered with a rug; a small tea table about eighteen inches square, standing about one foot above the floor, completed the necessary fitting of an oriental apartment. In the center of the house was a general reception and dining room containing a table and chairs. When more people came into my room than could be accommodated upon the divan, chairs were brought and then taken out when needed elsewhere. Simplicity characterizes every phase of oriental life, and if one enters into that life

VIEW OF MOUNT CARMEL AND THE SEA TAKEN FROM THE HOUSE WHERE BAHA'O'LLAH LIVED IN AKKA.

and adapts himself to the customs he will not find himself uncomfortable, for surely many of its customs are more adapted to the conditions there than would be transplanted westernisms.

As bedtime approached, I began mentally to make my arrangements for the night expecting to sleep upon the divan. However, as I was about to put this plan into effect, some of the friends appeared at the door with bundles of bedding which they proceeded to arrange in the following manner: A pashe-band (literally, mosquito box) was hung in the center of the chamber and sustained in place by cords to the four corners of the room. This contrivance is about six feet long by five in width and height. It is made of loosely woven cloth which admits the passage of air. In one end is an opening encircled by a draw-string; through this aperture the mattress and bedding are first inserted, then the sleeper crawls in, drawing the string after him. Inconvenient as this may seem, it is most comfortable and is absolute proof against vermin, including some of the larger and more dangerous species, such as scorpions and spiders, with which those eastern countries abound, the stings of which are always serious and sometimes fatal.

When the morning and the hour came for me to leave Akka, I was quite unconscious of it, being still lost in the realms of sleep. The previous day had been as strenuous a one as oriental conditions could have afforded; from five o'clock in the morning until eleven o'clock at night, almost without a break, I was conversing with various Believers, who had come to see me, so that when bedtime came I was tired out. Abdul-Baha came to say good-bye to me about half-past seven in the morning but, finding me still sleeping, would not allow me to be awakened, but stood guard at the door, walking up and down the narrow corridor. A half hour passed thus, when he was called out on the loggia which gave one of the Persian friends the watched-for opportunity to enter the room and give me a necessarily vigorous poking through the pashe-band, which aroused me. A half hour later I had received Abdul-Baha's fatherly embrace and parting blessing and, together with one of the oriental Bahais, was being driven through the canyon-like streets of Akka on the way to Haifa.

Abdul-Baha is anxious that in every possible way the believers in the East and West should unite; that communication should increase and that an interchange of ideas should ensue in order that all may profit thereby and be helped. Practically the only instruction which he gave me regarding my trip to Persia and Turkestan was that I should mingle freely with the Bahais and meet them on their own ground and in their own manner with a brother's embrace.

All who know Abdul-Baha love him devotedly, whether or not they be acquainted with the tenets of his teaching (on account of the oppression of the Bahais in the Holy Land and in the other Turkish countries until the present time practically no teaching has been done in those lands). One instance of this came to my immediate notice in the following way. Finding upon my return to Haifa from Akka that I had two days to wait for a steamer to take me on my journey, a young Persian Bahai who had been my constant companion and interpreter while in those parts, set out with me on an excursion to Nazareth. A drive of several hours across the plain of Kishon brought us to the mountains, high up in the valley of which is nestled the little town of Nazareth, the older parts of which have probably changed but little since the days of the Saviour, Jesus.

During the drive, my companion related several incidents of Bahai interest in connection with the places we were passing. He spoke in particular of one Sheikh Youseff, a man of wealth in lands and cattle, who formerly had lived in those parts and who, during the days when Baha'o'llah was there an exile, befriended and served Him in many ways. On arriving in Nazareth, we betook ourselves to call on the governor of the town, who was a son-in-law of the late sheikh. A very steep, narrow and dirty street flanked by high walls, brought us to the door of the governor's house which from without was unattractive enough. Upon entering, however, we found ourselves in a large court through which we were conducted to the principal reception room of the house, spacious, and beautifully furnished, the windows of which looked out over the receding terraced roofs of the neighboring houses, down the valley and on to the plain below. We were most graciously received by the governor. He spoke many times of his deep esteem and love for Abdul-Baha and, though he knew but little about

America and even less about the Bahai teaching, yet he was not at all surprised that Abdul-Baha should have so many friends in the far West, nor that these friends should travel over land and sea to spend ofttimes but a few hours with him. A servant was placed at our disposal to conduct us about the town to visit the many places of religious interest. Afterwards we visited the mausoleum of the late Sheikh Youseff, a beautiful marble structure, beneath the dome of which rested the sarcophagus of white marble overlaid with gold. Later, when we arrived at our hotel, we found a basket of fruit from the governor, and in the evening he came to return our call, and again, the next morning before our departure, sent one of his men in case we might need some service. These kindnesses to us, because we were friends of Abdul-Baha, spoke strongly of the esteem in which he is held by those outside of his following.

Embarking from Haifa in the evening, I landed the following morning shortly after sunrise in Beirut, the chief seaport of Syria, where I found a very hearty welcome at the hands of friends.

The kindness of one of these brothers was quite touching. He was a Jewish Bahai, originally from Hamadan, Persia, where there is a very large Israelitish following. He told me that sixteen years before he had wanted to go to America to teach the cause, but on account of not knowing the language, and for want of means, he had not been able to carry out his desire; nevertheless he had been constant in his prayers for the field of work in the West. Later on other teachers went to America and accomplished the work he had longed to do. How much work he had really done for America through prayer and earnest desire I could only judge from the love he had for the Bahais in the far West, of which I was the undeserving recipient. The significance of such a meeting is not understood at the time, but, after parting with such a friend, a touch of the spirit of brotherhood remains with one and causes one to realize the virtue of coming into contact with virtue.

Beirut is an important educational center and a number of Bahai young men are there as students. That night a meeting was held, attended mostly by these young believers, after which several of us supped together and repaired to the home of a Persian Bahai, formerly of Baghdad, where the night was spent. The city proper is built on a promontory projecting into the sea behind which rise abruptly the verdure-clad Lebanon Mountains whose summits are usually lost to view in the clouds. Our friend's house stood on a high point of land and from its terraced roof we had a superb view of the moonlit sea, the glittering shore of which stretched off to the south past the ancient towns of Tyre and Sidon and on toward the prison city of Akka, while, behind us, towered Lebanon, the twinkling lights of its many villas and villages giving a unique beauty to the scene.

Those who visit the Orient are always impressed by the brilliancy of its nights. Even the starlight there seems as brilliant as does the moonlight in more northern climes. To use an oriental expression, I will always have with me the "fragrance" of the nights spent on that rooftop during various visits to Beirut. Our host is now an old man. Since the days of The First Point (The Bab) he has been an ardent and faithful believer and has spent his life in serving the cause. Now his three sons are continuing his work and it is they who receive and serve the friends from the East and West as they pass through Beirut.

There is a poetry in oriental hospitality, which seems wanting in the western. Everything is so spontaneous and simple. Conversation with them is an art. Their narratives ramble along, always aiming, though indirectly, at a fixed point which is at first obscure, but which in the end they bring out with the accumulated force of many pictures and much action. Often the movement is not sufficiently accelerated to please our western craving for direct results—to see the end at the beginning—but nevertheless through it all runs a certain poetic strain, which is the spirit they wish to impart. This leaves the listener with a peculiar sense of being an actual part of that which is being related and he carries away with him a soul impression as well as the letter of the narrative. Imagine being on the roof-top of the house of our friend, the merchant of Baghdad, seated about a boiling samovar, sipping tea from small glass cups, while one of the sons relates events which transpired in the early days of the cause—those days when even to be suspected of being a believer was sufficient to have one's possessions confiscated

AGA SEYED TAGHI AFNAN AND TWO OF HIS SONS.

A BAHAI TRAVELLER

and possibly one's life forfeited. Under this terrible tyranny many of our people migrated from their homes to foreign parts, thus spreading the message far and wide. Such was the case of this family of Baghdad, who, after many troubles brought upon them by enemies of the faith, are now serving in a foreign land under more pacific conditions than before. It was in this house in Beirut that the friends sought refuge when several of them came overland from Persia in the winter with their precious burden, the blessed remains of The First Point, The Bab.

As is well known, after the martyrdom of The Bab in Tabriz His body was cast out into the moat which surrounded the city. Then it was that there arose a friend who went and recovered the remains, taking them to a place of safety and swathing them in tissues of silk. Afterwards they were secreted in one place for a time and then in other places known only to the faithful, and so many years passed. A few years ago, arrangements having been made for the entombment of The Bab's remains on Mount Carmel, two of the Bahais set out for Persia and, returning after a most eventful journey by camel across the desert with their holy burden, which was disguised as a bale of merchandise, reached the sea at Beirut, from whence the rest of the journey was made by water.

Though the steamer which I took from Beirut to Constantinople was not booked to sail until midday, yet in accordance with the oriental custom of arriving on board a steamer several hours ahead of time, I embarked in the early morning, several of the friends going in the bark to the steamer with me. Each of these arrived at the quay with a parting gift in his hand—a steamer chair, fruit, sweets, etc., a package of Persian insect powder (to the western mind a curious gift, but an article which adds much to the personal comfort of the traveler in those parts), and finally, after the party had left the ship, some one (I never knew who) sent me by a boatman a large jar of excellent potable water which was far superior to that afforded by the ship. I mention these details to show the extreme kindness of these friends—kindness to one whom many of them had not seen before nor probably would ever see again. This is indeed the spirit I have found manifest among the Bahais everywhere.

The passage from Beirut to Constantinople was uneventful, Smyrna, where the ship stopped for a few hours, being the only intermediate port. The Bahais in Syria had advised me not to land my luggage in Constantinople, but to continue passage by the same steamer to Odessa and from there on to Baku by rail. This was the route often taken by returning Bahai pilgrims, who dislike having anything more to do with the Turkish officials than is absolutely necessary.

Going ashore at Constantinople early in the morning I made my way to the abode of the American Bahai where my friend from whom I had parted in Vienna was staying. A hearty welcome, followed by a hasty meal, preceded our embarking, for our ship remained in port only a few hours. Until quite recently the oriental and occidental Bahais in Constantinople have been obliged to avoid meeting together on account of making trouble with the government, so during his visit there my friend had not been able to meet any of the eastern friends.

A cold and stormy passage of forty-eight hours across the Black Sea brought us to the port and city of Odessa. Here we took rail for Baku, a long ride, but one not devoid of interest. At first the line lay over rolling fields of grain-country, which reminded us much of our own western prairies—then, as the route turned off toward the south and we neared the Caucasus, we had splendid views of its rugged and picturesque mountain ranges towering in the distance one above the other. Again changing direction, the line bore off eastward and descended into the Caspian basin, where the railroad turns to the south following down the western coast to the sea, with an expanse of water stretching off to the right, the Caucasian Mountains rising abruptly on the left.

In Baku we had little difficulty in finding some of our Bahai friends. Fortunately for us, they were well known and easy to locate, for we did not speak a word of the language of the country. Here and in some other places in Southern Russia, as well as in Russian Turkestan, the Bahai movement and its followers are recognized and protected by the government. In fact, here we found that to be known as Bahais facilitated travel, for our people are known to be for peace and tranquility and are in no way associated with the many revolutionary movements which keep that country most of the time in a state of turbulence.

In Baku we were lodged in the house of a Bahai, Ashraff Karimoff, who lived only a few doors from the building now temporarily used as the Mashrak-el-Azcar.* Quite a large building-lot in the heart of the city has been acquired for the building of a Mashrak-el-Azcar. A building now standing in one corner of this property, besides serving as a place of meeting for the Bahais, affords lodging when traveling Bahais and their friends are entertained. Here also resides a Bahai teacher, who, with several other followers, serves the cause, thus forming an establishment which is the center of Bahai activities in that city.

During our stay in Baku, we were entertained several times by a Bahai, Aga Mussa Nagieff, a man who has extensive oil interests in that section. On the day following our arrival we went with him to inspect his oil wells at Bala Khaneh, not far from Baku. After spending some time among the wells we were taken to a house where a Bahai meeting had been arranged.

---

*Mashrak-el-Azcar means, literally, "The place of the mentions of God."

This meeting was composed chiefly of laboring men from the adjacent wells.

In the West many people are impressed by the fact that the Bahai teaching appeals alike to people of culture as well as to those who have not had the advantages of education and its responsibilities. This was even more striking in this meeting than any which I ever attended in the West. Several western travelers have written of the industries of Bala Khaneh and have described the way in which the oil is brought to the surface by the workmen, whose scanty clothing is saturated with unrefined petroleum. From this standpoint their condition is not enviable and needs to be improved, but we are permitted to see another aspect of their life which might astonish people in the West who to-day are striving to conciliate capital and labor. To see the capitalist and laborer side by side on equal terms in spirit in such a meeting as we had shows the work of the Bahai cause. Though in outward affairs there was a distinction between employer and employee, there was at the same time beneath that a fraternal relation which made their interests as one.

On another occasion we had an interesting

A BAHAI TRAVELLER 43

meeting with a number of Circassian peasants who came into the city from the country to greet us. The Circassian is a combination of several peoples, which gives him, along with the child-like simplicity and gentleness of the Oriental, a certain almost savage force which is characteristic of the north. It is ever interesting to witness the assimilation of these elements from the north, south, east and west by the Bahai faith, for wherever it is planted it finds root and grows.

From Baku our course of travel lay eastward over the Caspian into Turkestan. The afternoon of the evening that we left Baku a largely attended feast was spread in the Mashrak-el-Azcar. Tablets were chanted and my companion made an address in Persian which was translated for the benefit of those present into the language of the country. The meeting was brought somewhat abruptly to a close when one of the friends hurriedly entered to inform us that we had no time to lose in making our steamer. In almost less time than it takes to recount it the crowd had poured out into the street, where carriages awaited us, and amid good-byes, we, with as many others as the several vehicles would accommodate, were driven off rapidly toward the port.

On the quay and aboard the steamer we were met by others, the party growing as it was reinforced by groups of friends from the meeting, who arrived at intervals. Little did we think, as we stood on the stern of the moving steamer, waving adieu to the crowd on the pier, that there would be any annoying results from this farewell demonstration.

Turkestan, which is north of Persia, west of China, south of Russia and Siberia, and east of the Caspian Sea, has comparatively recently been opened to railroad travel by the Trans-Caspian line. The western extremity of this railroad is the town of Krasnovodsk, on the eastern coast of the Caspian. From here the line goes east to Eshkhabad, Merve, Samarkhand and Tashkhend; then northward to Orenberg, from whence a line joins it with the Trans-Siberian railroad.

On account of the proximity of Turkestan to India the Russians guard that country jealously. It is only by special permission that any foreigner is allowed to penetrate beyond the frontier. Before leaving America I tried

LAYING THE FOUNDATION OF THE MASHRAK EL-AZCAR IN ESHKHABAD.

A BAHAI TRAVELLER

to inform myself of these matters through the Russian embassy in Washington, from which I was able to obtain no information at all. While in Europe I applied to the American ambassador in St. Petersburg, asking him to procure for my friend and me the necessary permission to travel as tourists in Turkestan. In reply to this I was notified by letter and by wire that the necessary permission had been granted and that while no document was sent us, the officials along the Trans-Caspian route had been advised of our coming.

On the steamer from Baku we met two Bahais with their families, who were traveling our way, so we consolidated into one party. On arriving at Krasnovodsk the following morning we landed and, finding that our train did not leave until late in the afternoon, we made ourselves comfortable under the shade of some trees in a garden adjoining the station. Seated here we had lunch and, later on, tea. We were about to collect our luggage for boarding the train when we were approached by a police officer accompanied by two men who demanded to see our papers. This, of course, was no more than travelers in those countries expect at any time, so we were troubled only when told that there was no permission for us to travel in those parts and that we would be detained there until such had been received.

It was with some degree of consternation that we watched the train pulling out with our Persian friends aboard, and then we turned to survey the town about us. It was about as barren a place as the imagination could have conceived. Hemmed in by the sea against mountains as barren as only the salt wastes of the Caspian basin can be, the only verdure being a few trees and shrubs which had to be watered with distilled sea water—there was no fresh water within miles—Krasnovodsk was indeed uninviting for an indefinite sojourn such as ours bade fair to be.

The officer who had jurisdiction over us was politeness itself. Even under the most exasperating circumstances he was all smiles and would bow most gallantly with his right hand placed over his heart. We were lodged in a hotel where he lived and, though a sharp eye was kept upon us, we were at liberty to wander about the town as we chose.

As soon as possible we wired to our ambassador in St. Petersburg and also to the military

A BAHAI TRAVELLER 47

governor of Tashkhend, under whose governorship is the government of Western Turkestan, asking them to take steps for us to be allowed to continue our journey.

On the third day of our stay, when we were beginning to weary of the monotony of waiting, the door of our room opened and in walked three Bahais from Eshkhabad—Mirza Taghi Khan, Mirza Housein Oskoui and Mirza Fazl'o'llah Khan. Before then we had been in telegraphic communication with the friends in Eshkhabad, and knowing of our plight these three friends had come down a run of eighteen hours to Krasnovodsk to share with us the period of waiting. They told us that the Bahais in Eshkhabad had been advised of our expected arrival in their city by dispatch from Baku, and about fifty of them came a four-hours' journey down the line to meet us. There in a small station house they spent the day and night expecting us by every train.

The remainder of our time in Krasnovodsk passed comparatively quickly. On the fifth day in the afternoon a dispatch came from the military governor of the province granting the waited-for permission. It was with much hilarity that we hastily gathered our belongings together and, within the hour, were boarding the train for Eshkhabad.

Only after the affair was over did we ascertain the real cause of our detention. It seems that the police in Baku witnessed our departure from that city, and imagining from the parting demonstration that we might be political agitators, telegraphed to Krasnovodsk and, though we had the necessary permission to travel in Transcaspia, it was cancelled by this dispatch. Unpleasant as this affair seemed at the time it was indeed a very good thing in the end, for the people of Krasnovodsk were impressed by the fact that two Bahais were there from America and in this way our three oriental friends who spoke the language of the country were able to do quite a little teaching.

The route to Eshkhabad was over the desert. For the most part of the way we were in sight of the Sagir mountains on the south, which here form the northern boundary of Persia. On the following morning, drawing nearer to this range, we began to distinguish, by the streaks of verdure on the mountain sides, rivulets coming down to be absorbed by the thirsty sands of the plain. Every few miles could be seen the remains of ruined cities. In a recent tablet revealed to the Bahais of the East and of the West Abdul-Baha mentions this country in the following terms:

"For man has two aspects—one the sublimity of nature and intellectual qualities, and the other the base animality and imperfections of passion.

"If you travel through the continents and countries of the world you will see on one side the signs of ruin and destruction, and on the other the signs and monuments of civilization and construction. As to the ruin and destruction, they are the signs of contention and discord, of war and battle. But order and construction are the results of the virtues of friendliness and concord.

"If one travel in the central desert of Asia he will observe how many great and populous cities have been ruined. From the Caspian Sea to the River Oxus naught is to be seen save forlorn and deserted prairies and deserts. The Russian Railway [the Trans-Caspian R. R.] takes two days and two nights to traverse the ruined cities and destroyed villages of that desert. There was a time when that land was very populous and in the highest state of civilization and development; science and knowledge were widespread, the arts and professions established, commerce and agriculture were in the utmost state of perfection, and civil government and politics well organized. Now, all this great region is the habitation of desolation and shelters only the nomadic Turkoman tribes and the wandering beasts of prey. The cities of that land, as Ghorgan, Tassa, Abiavard, and Shahrastan, were once famous in the world for sciences, knowledge, professions, wonders, wealth, greatness, happiness and virtue. Now no voice or murmur is to be heard in all that land save the roar of ferocious brutes, and naught is to be seen save the wandering wolves.

"This ruin and destruction was occasioned by the battles and wars between Iran (Persia) and Turkan, which had become different in customs and religion. Their godless leaders made public property of the blood, belongings, and the privacy of each other. This is the exposition of one instance.

"Then, when ye travel through the world and observe it, ye shall find all constructiveness and progressiveness to be signs of friendliness and

A BAHAI TRAVELLER

love, and all destructiveness and ruin the results of hatred and enmity."

Before leaving Krasnovodsk our companions had telegraphed ahead to Eshkhabad and various intermediate points to announce our coming, so at a very early hour the next morning we began to be greeted by groups of Bahais gathered at the stations along the line. The people aboard the train eyed us with no little interest, for it was uncommon to say the least to see foreigners so received. At two hours or more from Eshkhabad we were met by a delegation of believers from that city, who brought to us the greeting of their assembly.

The climax was reached when the train finally pulled into the station at Eshkhabad, where three hundred and more of the friends awaited us. As we stood on the platform of the car looking down into a sea of upturned faces, with many hands stretched out towards us, a wave of sympathy came over me which was difficult to stand up against; but then was no time to break down, so with an effort I collected myself and stepped down into the crowd. Before I could realize it, I found myself hurried through the station with several hands upon each of my arms. Outside many carriages were in waiting, and without the loss of a moment we were being driven at a seemingly dangerous rate of speed toward the Mashrak-el-Azcar.

The Mashrak-el-Azcar of Eshkhabad—the largest structure of its kind so far erected—stands in about the center of the city, with its roof and dome rising high above the surrounding houses and trees. It is visible for miles over the plain as the traveler approaches the city, and seems only more imposing than from afar when one finds himself within its enclosure. Here, in the lower loggia which surrounds the building, we were greeted individually by several hundred Bahais. After tea and cooling drinks had been served and greetings exchanged, everything quieted down while prayers were chanted. During this service all present sat in a respectful attitude, while one of the friends, the possessor of a rich and melodious voice, lifted it in chants of praise and thanksgiving. We were indeed thankful to have attained the blessing of this meeting.

The chanting over, the meeting broke up and we were then taken around the temple on a tour of inspection. Going up into the building almost

THE MASHRAK-EL-AZCAR OF ESHKHABAD UNDER CONSTRUCTION.

A BAHAI TRAVELLER

to the top of the dome, we had a fine view of the town with its many gardens and surrounding country. The town was as a green oasis in the desert, water from the neighboring mountains being brought to the city and conducted through water-ways to the various parks and gardens and along the gutters, in order that even the trees which flank the streets might be watered.

In the days of Baha'o'llah, He advised certain Bahais to migrate to and settle in Eshkhabad.* At that time the place was little more than a huddle of mud huts. However, little by little, broad boulevards were laid off and substantial houses were erected in place of the former inferior ones, until now it is a modern and prosperous city.

The Mashrak-el-Azcar stands in the center of a garden bounded by four streets. In the four corners of this enclosure are four buildings. One is the Bahai school; one is the mosaferkhaneh, or travelers' house, where pilgrims and travelers are lodged; one is for the keepers, while the fourth one is to be used as a hospital. Nine radial avenues approach the temple from the sev-

---
*Eshkhabad means "City of Love."

eral parts of the grounds, one of which, the principal approach to the building, leads from the main gateway of the grounds to the principal portal of the temple.

The temple is built on the plan of a regular polygon of nine sides. One side is occupied by the main entrance, flanked by two slender turrets. This, the principal doorway, opens toward the direction of the Holy Land. The entire building is surrounded by two series—one upper and one lower—of loggias which open out upon the garden.

The principal feature of the interior is the rotunda beneath the dome, which latter is the dominant feature of the exterior. The rotunda is surrounded by an aisle or ambulatory. Doors give egress from the ambulatory to the lower loggia without.

The interior walls of the rotunda are treated in five distinct stories. First, a series of nine arches and piers which separate the rotunda from the ambulatory. Second, a similar treatment with balustrades which separate the triforium gallery (which is above the ambulatory and is reached by two staircases in the loggias, placed one on either side of the main entrance) from the well of the rotunda. Third, a series of nine blank arches filled with fretwork, between which are escutcheons bearing The Greatest Name.* Fourth, a series of nine large arched windows. Fifth, a series of eighteen bull's-eye windows. Above and resting on a cornice surmounting this last story rises the inner hemispherical shell of the dome.

The interior is elaborately decorated in plaster relief work. I am under the impression that eventually it is the intention to treat the interior in colors and gold, but at present it is in the simple white stucco. The exterior is also being done in stucco, which in that climate resists quite well the action of the elements. The style of the temple is oriental, such as is common in Persia, while the exterior treatment of certain parts reminds one of the famous Taj-Mahal in India. The walls, which are of brick, are massively built, while the floors and dome are of concrete and iron. The whole structure impresses one by its mass and strength.

Imposing as is the Mashrak-el-Azcar as a building, the symbol for which it stands, the spiritual unity of the Bahais of the Orient, is

---
*Allaho'Abha (God is the Most Glorious).

that which impresses the believer more than all else. It represents the voluntary heartfelt offerings of a multitude of souls, the blending of the spirit of which is a power distinctively felt. The temple building is as an ensign which testifies of this unity.

That which is manifested or expressed is more virile and forceful than that which is not manifested or unexpressed. The rearing of this temple in the East has been a great source of strength to the people there, for through thus expressing their unity the Bahais have become stronger and more united than ever before. Now in America the Bahais are arising to build a Mashrak-el-Azcar. Who can estimate the effect which will be produced by this building? It will be the cause of great strength and unity among the believers of the Occident and, being The House of Unity open to all peoples, it will be as a haven of rest to many a soul and as a beacon to guide those who seek. This all and more, too, it will be for us of the West. Now for those faithful souls of the Orient—those through whose suffering and sacrifice we in the West have received the spiritual light of this latter-day revelation—those through whose labors the

A BAHAI TRAVELLER

way has been made easy for us of the Occident —a Mashrak-el-Azcar in America will be as the confirmation of their hopes and prayers for the West.

The erection of a temple in the West will strengthen the Holy Cause in the East more than anything which could happen in this country. Has not Abdul-Baha said that after teaching the Message of Baha'o'llah of all things now to be accomplished in the West the building of the temple is the most important? Throughout the Bahai world the eyes of all are expectingly turned toward this country. Now we must show them a sign of spiritual unity and this must be the Mashrak-el-Azcar.

The Bahais of Eshkhabad form a strong element in the life of the place, and they are highly thought of and protected by the government. One of the friends told us of the way in which—about eighteen or twenty years ago—the Bahai Cause was first brought to the public notice in Eshkhabad by a martyrdom. It was the case of a learned man of some prominence, who met his death through receiving many wounds at the hands of two assassins. These two individuals had been hired to do the deed by five Moslems, who took this measure to try to stop the spread of the cause in that city. The Russian authorities took the matter in hand and condemned to death all seven men. The Bahais then petitioned the governor to spare their lives. He not having authority to do this, a petition to the same effect was sent to the Czar, who granted it, and thus the prisoners were sent in chains to the mines of Siberia and now not one of the seven remains. Here is but another instance of the growth of the cause through persecution, for from that time on the government not only allowed the Bahais to worship as they chose, but it protected them and showed them special favors.

During our stay in Eshkhabad we were entertained in the home of a Bahai by the name of Abbasoff. The house with its terrace, porches and garden was a large one, but none too spacious for the number of friends who thronged it. Sometimes we sat at table with as many as forty persons, and I do not recall dining with less than fifteen at table. Between meals the samovar was constantly kept boiling and a running service of tea, ices and cooling drinks was for the refreshment of the many callers.

Three days after our arrival in Eshkhabad we

went up into the mountains for a few days to a resort called Feerouzay, where some of our friends had summer homes. Several of the Bahais accompanied us thither, and while there we were joined by about thirty others who had gone up from the city for the occasion.

Every arrangement was made for our personal comfort during the drive of several hours to Feerouzay. We halted several times beside streams to rest the horses as well as to refresh ourselves by washing our faces and hands. In those oriental countries there is much dust, so the traveler welcomes running water. In one of the carriages was a supply of ice and soda waters —nothing had been forgotten. At first the route lay over a track on the sandy plain as far as the mountains, then it wound up a narrow gorge until a fertile valley high up in the mountains was reached, at the upper end of which was the town of Feerouzay.

In the bazaar quarter of the town we were greeted by a number who had congregated there to welcome us. They were arranged in a double line on either side of the roadway as we drove past. Shortly after our arrival in the home of Mirza Mohammed Afnan, a son of the aged

Afnan of Akka, where we were to be entertained, quite a party gathered for dinner, the festivity continuing late into the night.

During the drive up to Feerouzay, my companion fell into conversation with the driver of the carriage in which he rode, and the man became much interested in the teaching. On the following day, at an early hour, the latter came with his family to the house to see my friend and to hear more about the message. Our coming had been noised about, so we met many others, also, who were desirous of knowing about the Bahai teaching.

From where we were, near the frontier, we could see the mountains of Persia. It seemed strange that upon one side of an imaginary line our people were protected and safe, while, upon the other side, opposite conditions reigned. The Bahais are safe in Turkestan, so from time to time Bahai refugees have sought protection there from the persecutions in Persia. Sheikh Ali Akbar, one of the friends who formerly had been a mullah (priest of Islam), told us of some of the troubles which he had encountered through preaching and teaching among his own people, until finally he had been obliged to leave his

A GROUP OF BAHAIS IN KHAZVIN.

A BAHAI TRAVELLER

home. This man interested us greatly—a man of commanding presence, whose finely cut features and poise of bearing bespoke the high caste Moslem with his pride and learning, in addition to which was the gentle influence of love which had come into his life with his acceptance of the Bahai faith and his trouble and sacrifices therein. A whole history was written in the lines of his face.

Another type was Sheikh Mohammed Ali, upon whom devolves the chanting of the prayers and holy words in the Mashrak-el-Azcar, who has been given this service to perform on account of his vocal qualifications and devotion to the cause. From his brilliant face, smiles and good cheer, one could hardly believe that his back and shoulders were a mass of scars from wounds inflicted as torture for his faith at the hands of fanatical Moslems.

Everywhere we found joy upon the faces of those who had suffered the most. Only once do I recall encountering grief. It was upon meeting with a believer, a very old and infirm man, who wept when he greeted us. We were told that several members of his family had been martyred during the comparatively recent massacres of Bahais in Yazd.

While in Feerouzay there was a constant round of meetings and gatherings. I will make special mention of one—a Bahai christening which we attended. On the day of our arrival in Eshkhabad a son was born to Aga Reza, one of the friends of Feerouzay. We were asked to name the baby. My friend selected the name Rouh'o'llah, which gave evident satisfaction. On the fifth day after the child's birth we all gathered at the house where a feast had been prepared. Tables were spread on a broad piazza overlooking a garden. The baby was brought out held up for inspection, prayers and tablets were chanted, and before the refreshments were served a translation of one of *Mrs. Waite's poems was also chanted.

Unfortunately we were limited as to time and were unable to travel further into Turkestan, where there are other Bahai centers. While in Eshkhabad we met several friends from Merve, Samarkhand and Khokhand (which latter is the extreme eastern end of Turkestan near the confines of China), and it was difficult to resist the

---
*One of the American Bahais.

urgent and pressing invitations to visit their cities.

Our departure from Eshkhabad was as much of an occasion as our arrival had been. It seemed as if every person we had met while there was at the station to bid us adieu. Then, at several stations along the route of travel, we were again met by the same good friends who had welcomed us before. Three of our good oriental brothers accompanied us from Eshkhabad to Baku, where we arrived after two nights and one day of travel.

The two days spent in Baku, between our second arrival and our departure for Persia, passed in much the same way as had our previous visit. We were constantly with the friends and on the move from one meeting or entertainment to the next. Quite the same crowd escorted us again to the quay, this time there being no possibility of the authorities making trouble for us, as we were to land upon Persian—not Russian—soil.

In going from Russia into Persia the Bahai is struck by the difference in the outward attitude in relation to the cause of the friends in those two countries. In Russia they are outspoken about the faith, because they are protected, while in Persia it is often with difficulty that one is able to recognize the Bahais, because they dare not always manifest their real selves on account of the persecution. One instance of this happened on board the steamer from Baku as she was entering Persian waters.

Before sailing we were told that there were some spies aboard and, in case we were questioned as to our business, to be careful with our replies. Consequently, when I was approached by a tall young man wearing a Russian cap and long military coat, who persisted in questioning me regarding my sojourn in Baku and my destination and friends in Persia, I intimated as plainly as possible, without actually telling him so, that I did not desire his company. Nevertheless, he pushed the matter by asking if I did not know various people in Baku, mentioning certain Bahais who lived there. Something, either in my reply or perhaps in my evasion of his question, seemed to give him the cue he sought. We were seated at a table on the deck of the steamer, and reaching under the table he grasped my hand, at the same time pronouncing The Greatest Name, the Bahai greeting—"Allaho'Abha" My chagrin at having so sedulously tried to avoid this man was only counteracted by the pleasure of meeting him as a friend and brother. We had supper together, followed by a conversation which lasted late into the night. He was a student of engineering in a college in Baku and was then taking a vacation trip into Persia. Before the steamer reached Enzalee, where we landed, our friend had disembarked at an intermediate port on his way into the interior.

The contrast between the eastern and southern shores of the Caspian Sea is most striking. The former, or that of Turkestan, is arid and sterile, while the latter, or that of Persia, is most luxuriantly clothed with verdure. As the steamer neared the coast the very air teemed with vegetation and insect life. The sea being very shallow about Enzalee, in rough weather vessels have difficulty in making the port. Fortunately for us there was no sea on, so the landing was easily accomplished.

Mirza Taghi Khan, who had accompanied us from Eshkhabad, recognized a Bahai brother in the custom-house office, where we had some formalities to attend to in entering our luggage, but it not being advisable there to enter into salutations and conversation with this friend, we simply exchanged fraternal and understanding glances and passed on.

From Enzalee we re-embarked for Peere Bazaar en route for Resht—a trip of three or four hours. The boat was rowed and poled across the lagoons, which here begin near the sea coast, extending inland for some distance. After a time we entered an inlet, whereupon the crew descended to a towpath and towed the craft to the bazaar where we landed.

I wish I might adequately describe this boat ride. It was so typical of Persia that nothing could have formed a better introduction to that country and to her people. The absolute simplicity of the mode of transportation, with the absence of all hustle and bustle, made it seem quite like a pleasure excursion where time was no object whatever.

On the stern of the boat was constructed a rude framework upon which was stretched an awning under which, reclining on cushions, we made ourselves comfortable. The lagoon was bordered by thickets of reeds and rushes, and at several points we saw buffaloes feeding on rushes, their great black hairless backs protruding from the water, giving them the appearance of amphibious monsters.

As we entered the inlet we passed close to huddles of huts, where we were able to obtain a first glimpse of the domestic life of the country people. Here in the lowlands, where timber is plenty, the houses of the poorer people are built of a light hewn timber framework, which is thatched and walled with reeds and rushes and, in some cases, plastered with mud. On account of the humidity of the marshes the floor is usually raised several feet above the ground, allowing a circulation of air beneath the house.

We were rather rudely awakened from this dreamlike atmosphere of simple life and poetic travel by the confusion which accompanied our landing at Peere Bazaar. Surrounded by a score of men, each of whom laid hold of at least one of our many articles of impediment, we made our way up a steep bank to a large building which housed the shops of the bazaar. After a heated discussion of some length with a carriage driver —a discussion in which each member of the assembled crowd took great interest—a bargain was made, so we mounted and began the drive toward the city of Resht, only a few miles distant.

On the highroads of Persia one sees almost every aspect of the life of the people of the lower classes. At every turn and between the turns are tchi khanehs or tea houses, where the people gather to partake of tea, their national beverage. These buildings always have large doorways opening toward the road, and, in some cases, even the whole side of the house is formed of movable shutters, which, when removed, give the house the character of a great porch. Against the wall, usually opposite the doorway, is the sakkou, a stand upon which rests the samovar or tea urn. This stand is often quite an elaborate affair, somewhat resembling a church altar with its series of steps and shelves, upon which are displayed lamps, tea utensils and the like, which form the necessary culinary outfit of the establishment. On a broad, low seat extending about the walls of the room sit, in the Persian fashion, with their feet drawn up under them, the customers drinking their tea, and smoking their large water pipes. Here often a minstrel is heard singing his lay to an accompaniment played upon a guitar-like instrument, while ofttimes professional story-tellers or travelers entertain the crowd with tales and anecdotes. The Persian is undoubtedly the most social of all men, and this characteristic is the first and last impressed upon the traveler as he journeys through the country, for he observes it in every grade of society.

On arriving in Resht, we drove to the house of one of the Bahai friends. The master of the house was not at home, but after we explained to the servants that we had come for a visit they made us very welcome, serving a lunch, after which, according to the custom of the country, we were put to bed for an afternoon nap. After sleeping for an hour or more I awoke, and looking out into the next room, saw there our host quietly seated waiting for us to awake. Though I had never met this good friend I recognized him from having seen his photograph, and on going out into the next room he greeted me with the hospitable and customary embrace of the Orient.

Our thought had been to stay at Resht only over night, but when we found ourselves in the hands of the friends there it was difficult to break away. After much talking they decided to allow us to continue our journey at the expiration of three days.

In the late afternoon of the day we arrived, we began to receive calls from friends who had been notified of our arrival. On account of the persecution of our people in Resht not more than nineteen or twenty gathered in the house at any one time, but there was a constant coming and going until late in the night. Everyone was anxious to hear the latest news from Akka and also of the work in the West. My companion, who spoke the language of the country, was kept quite busy talking. Not speaking Persian, my conversation was limited to the few who spoke English and French. However, this was not without its advantages, for not being occupied in talking, I had an opportunity for observing many things which otherwise might have escaped me.

After dinner, which was served between ten and eleven o'clock at night, we mounted to a balcony overlooking the neighboring houses and gardens, where coffee was served. Here we sat talking of the cause until a late hour. The stillness of the nights in the Orient is impressive.

Here we were in the heart of a large city, yet save for the occasional cry of a night watchman, or a singer chanting, or the tinkling of the bells of a caravan passing in the distance, there was nothing to break the silence. This, with the brilliancy of the firmament and the refreshing breezes of the night in contrast with the parching heat of the day, makes the night the time when the Oriental people really live.

Under such climatic conditions it is not surprising that the Oriental has turned his attention from things material to things immaterial, from the practical to the poetic, and from the outer world of nature to the inner world of the spirit. Things spiritual have always had their first fruition and growth in the Orient and from there they have found their way to the West, where they have become the moving factor in our lives and the basis of our civilization.

It was in Persia that the wise men of old read from the heavens of the approaching birth of Jesus, The Christ, before they went westward to welcome and pay homage to Him, the Messiah. It was from the Orient that Christ's message went forth to the western world—the fruits of the spirit of which we in the West are now enjoying—for the most enlightened civilization of the present day is the fruit of the spiritual awakening of man through Christ.

But now another note has sounded throughout the world. Baha'o'llah, the Promised One of all religions, has appeared in order to unite all peoples of all faiths, and it was with His followers that we lived and traveled in the East. Surely no western travelers in those distant lands ever had so warm a reception as we did—at times entertained in the places of the wealthy, and at other times in the simplest of mud dwellings along the wayside; yet everywhere with the same heartfelt hospitality. The fact that one was able to serve a banquet, and another but a cup of tea, in no way seemed to restrict the warmth of the meeting nor their desire to share with others.

With the Bahais the tie of faith is the strongest of ties. Though two Bahais may meet but for a few moments it is as if they had always been friends. Westerners have written and said much about the treachery of the Oriental, while but scanty if any mention is made of him as a friend. Westerners see the wrong side of Eastern character, because they usually go to the

A GROUP OF MOSLEM BAHAIS IN TEHERAN.

East to plunder—not to court—for most times they go to the East to enrich themselves at the expense of the Oriental. This is easy and possible because of the superior practical education of the West but, in turn, it has its reactionary effect upon both peoples, for it increases the natural abyss between Occident and Orient and calls forth the worst characteristics of both. But how different is all this with those who go to the East in the Bahai spirit of brotherhood to give and to win and not to take. They find friends in every city and hamlet, and many a friendly door open to them along the roadside and caravan route, for through the uniting spirit of the Bahai teaching, the greatest degree of fraternity and friendship exists among its followers. Through this spiritual power the highest and most noble characteristics of man's soul are developed and become his ruling instincts.

The three days spent in Resht passed quickly. Here we had our first glimpse of the home life of the people of Persia, for we were with the friends all the time, going from one home to the next, for a meal here or for tea there. We always met small groups of people, wisdom not permitting the holding of large gatherings on account of the opposition and trouble brought about by the unbelievers. I recall one day when we had gathered, nineteen in number, in the upper part of a dwelling. The friend who chanted the prayers and holy verses used caution in modulating his voice, so that it might not carry to the street below, lest it might attract the attention of unfriendly ears. During this meeting a commotion took place in the street beneath. This was caused by an altercation between some passers-by. For a moment every one in the chamber held his breath, until one of the men, cautiously approaching a window, satisfied himself that there was no danger. I will never forget this picture. The assembled Believers exchanged glances which bespoke experiences of past troubles and persecutions, while at the far end of the room stood the friend cautiously peering out into the street through the partially closed shutter.

Much suffering and trouble has made the Persian Bahais vigilant and cautious in evading the troubles heaped upon them by the Musselmans, yet at the same time it has made them strong in faith and ready to withstand the most dire ca-

A BAHAI TRAVELLER

lamity and even martyrdom in the cause. Once I remonstrated with some friends against their being seen walking in the streets with my companion and me, lest this should cause trouble for them whereupon, not understanding me very well, they assured me that no bodily harm could befall us because we were Occidentals, for whom even the fanatical Moslems have a certain respect, while, as for themselves, they were ready at all times to be added to the great army of Bahai martyrs. Though dispassionately said, they but voiced the sentiment of the Persian Bahais in general, the sincerity of which has often been demonstrated by the vast numbers who willingly and with joy have sacrificed property, family and life in the path of Baha.

Teheran is about two hundred and twenty-five miles from Resht by the carriage road. This road, built and maintained by Russian enterprise, is an excellent piece of engineering, and in recent years has made the trip to the capital one of comparative ease and comfort. A well organized system of relay stations affords changes of horses along the route, so if the traveler be pressed for time the entire trip may be made in forty-eight or fifty hours. However, this traveling day and night without rest is fatiguing, so we found it better to travel by night, resting in the middle of the day when the sun was highest.

Accordingly, my American companion, Mirza Taghi Khan, our Persian friend, and I set out from Resht for Teheran. Several of the good friends accompanied us to a point without the city limits, where we changed from the light carriage in which we had come to a heavy traveling coach drawn by four horses, which was to convey us to our destination. Here parting greetings were exchanged and we started on our cross-country journey.

For some distance our way led through the rice fields of the lowlands which border the Caspian Sea and where the sea once extended until driven back by alluvial deposits brought down from the mountains. Then, winding up a broad valley, we found ourselves amid the heavily wooded foot hills of the Elburz range. Making stops every three or four hours to change horses gave us opportunity to refresh ourselves with tea and food at the post-khanehs (post-houses) along the route.

At various points we were met by Bahai friends who had been notified of our coming. At one place a friend was very disappointed that we could not remain for dinner, but as we had dined shortly before, it was impossible and we did not have time to remain until the next meal. To our surprise, a few hours later, while stopping at a post-khaneh we had a phone message from an inn a couple of hours ahead saying that our friend, with whom we were not able to dine, had arranged by phone that we should be his guests there that evening, even though he could not be there to feast with us. The object of the message sent us from the inn was to inquire what we might like for dinner in order that all might be in readiness when we arrived.

In one place I well remember we were met by a young man who had lived in Shiraz. He took us into his little house consisting of but one room. Simple as was this abode we had no more hearty welcome anywhere. Searching in the depths of a chest he produced pamphlets and Bahai greetings printed in Washington, which had found their way thither and were being preserved along with other treasures relating to the cause. Here we remained for tea, but as our time was limited, we felt we must decline a very pressing invitation to remain for the night. Our young friend, disappointed at not seeing more of us, took the fourth place in the coach and journeyed along with us in order that the visit might be prolonged.

Shortly before our arrival in Persian territory, the country had been greatly stirred by the bombardment of the parliament in Teheran by the troops of the Shah, and of the massacre and imprisonment of a number of the members of that unfortunate body. This action upon the part of the imperial party was the outcome of a long disagreement between the Shah and the Constitutionalists—a political matter which for some time had agitated the country.

As we journeyed onward, our friend spoke at some length of these political troubles which were occupying the attention of every one, at the same time saying that the Bahais had remained neutral in the hope of helping the condition of the country along the lines of peace and arbitration rather than by strife and bloodshed. Later on he informed us that several constitutionalist fugitives, on their way from Teheran to exile in Europe, were hourly expected to pass over that

A BAHAI TRAVELLER

portion of the route; so we kept an eye ahead, hoping to obtain a glimpse of the expected party.

By this time the road had entered between high and barren mountains with scarcely a vestige of vegetation, for we were leaving behind us the fertile lowlands and ascending the mountains which form the northern buttress of the great central plateau of Persia. To add to the dismalness of the scene night was closing in and gusts of wind mingled with rain and flashes of lightning made the falling darkness more intense, while peals of distant thunder broke the monotony of the clatter of the horses' hoofs and the rumble of the coach.

More and more the mountain sides encroached upon the valley, until the road entered a deep gorge in the rocks. To one side towered an almost perpendicular cliff; on the other descended a chasm, in the depths of which dashed a mountain torrent on its turbulent way to the lands below. While passing through this defile, the pent-up fury of the storm broke with all its force. Suddenly a shout was heard ahead, and we peered out into the gloom just in time to see three coaches pass in quick succession. With the first came a flash of lightning that revealed to us the anxious and haggard faces of its occupants—two of the fugitives in their flight. In an instant they were gone, and the noise of the coaches was lost in the distance.

In a few moments a bridge over the ravine and an abrupt turn in the road brought us out into a broad upland valley, where the storm had ceased, and shortly we drew up before the house of a Bahai friend in the village of Mangile, to find a welcome awaiting us. Here we took refuge, and in an upper chamber seated ourselves about a table upon which was spread a tempting meal.

After supper we sat talking for a time and listening to some music which our friend, who had lived in Shiraz, made upon a Persian guitar. Being tired, both the other American and I fell asleep. Awaking about three hours later, we found the sky perfectly clear and the world bathed in the brilliant moonlight of the East. So, parting with our good host and the young man who had accompanied us thither, we set out again upon our journey, refreshed in body and soul by the hospitality and the affectionate meeting with these Bahai brothers.

The ancient city of Khazvin is the only place of importance between Resht and Teheran. It being one of the principal Bahai centers of Persia, we planned to tarry there in order to meet the Believers. About four hours from the city, we stopped at a post-khaneh to sleep and rest, for we knew that on arrival in a Bahai community we would be much feted and have little opportunity for repose.

As soon as we had settled ourselves in the inn, the sound of carriages entering the court yard announced the arrival of other guests. Surveying the newcomers from a window, I counted eight men as they descended from two carriages. Suddenly I recognized one of the number, a certain physician of Khazvin with whom I had corresponded and whose features I recalled from having seen several photographs of him. These friends, hearing of our approach, hastily joined themselves into a party, coming over the road to meet us. The greeting was a hearty one. Our friends had not come empty handed, for, as soon as the first salutations were over, trays of delicious fruits were produced, tea was served, and thus we spent an hour or more in conversation and feasting.

While during very recent years the Bahais have been comparatively tranquil in Khazvin, nevertheless, even now, great care has to be observed and every precaution is taken against giving people the slightest ground to criticise or make trouble for the Believers. Accordingly, two hours before dusk we all set out for the city, entering the gates under cover of the night. After wending our way through many narrow and tortuous streets, some lined with shops and brilliantly lighted, others flanked by high walls and dark, we found ourselves at the house of the Bahai doctor.

A small, low, and heavily-barred doorway, piercing a massive brick wall, formed the street entrance to the house. On entering, we found ourselves in a small court-yard lighted by many lamps, about which were placed plants and shrubs in tubs and pots. Behind this, to one side, opened a large court containing a garden, while, upon the other side was the entrance to the house. Entering the latter, and halting for a few moments in an antechamber to remove the dust from our clothing and wash our hands and faces at a small fountain placed there for the purpose, we were taken to the guest room. As soon as we arrived, friends began to call in small groups, coming and going until dinner was served, which, according to the custom of the place, was just before bed time. After dinner we went to our room and, tired by travel and the social events of the day, we fell asleep, not awaking until the sun was quite high.

To the Oriental, all hours of the twenty-four are the same. He is quite as apt to have a caller at sunrise as at sunset, and he thinks nothing of starting forth on a cross-country journey at one or two o'clock in the night. When we awoke about eight o'clock the morning after our arrival in Khazvin, we found several friends assembled to see us, while, to our chagrin, we learned that others had come and, not able to remain, had gone while we slept. As in other places, our stay here was one continuous round of visits, something being planned for every hour of the day. On our first afternoon we were entertained at tea at the house of a certain Bahai merchant. This meeting was so typically Persian and picturesque in its setting, that I must give a brief description of it.

Escorted by some of the friends, we went through narrow streets until we came to the house of the merchant. A simple doorway in a wall of sun-dried and burnt bricks opened on a flight of steps, which descended to the level of the outer court-yard of the house. Crossing this court, in the center of which was a basin of water surrounded by flowers, we were taken by an exterior staircase to the upper floor of the house, and passing through an antechamber, we entered the room where the friends awaited us.

I will never forget the first impression of this meeting. Imagine a large room with a low paneled ceiling, a long table a mass of color with its fruits and viands, while the air was filled with a fragrance of flowers placed about in profusion, broad open windows, the transoms of which were filled with intricate fretwork and colored glass, looking down upon a series of gardens that stretched off toward the country, with a background of distant mountains; then, in the midst of this beautiful and harmonious scene, forty or more Bahais seated about the room in their many colored robes—it was a picture never to be forgotten.

Men of all ages were there. Some who, after many years of hardship and service in the cause, were entering into the evening of this life, while others, young and in full vigor of manhood, were in the prime of their time of service. I well remember two—father and son—the older man, blind and feeble in body, yet with a keen mind and an enthusiastic soul, while his son, strong in body, was eyes and limbs for his father. Thus they had traveled together and taught in many towns and provinces and were at that time teaching in Khazvin.

We were given seats at the head of the table and after the usual service of chanting, feasting commenced with an interchange of ideas and items of Bahai interest, both occidental and oriental. After the feast we took a stroll through the garden, and at dusk, bidding adieu to our host and his guests we returned to the house of the good hakim (physician).

Even in the earliest days of the holy cause Khazvin was an important center. Kurratu'l-Ayn, to whom The Bab gave the title Jenab-i-Tahira (Her Highness, the Most Pure), was of Khazvin. Her fame as a poetess, as a heroine and a servant in the days of The Bab, and as a martyr in the cause, is well known amongst the Bahai friends. It is in the garden of her house in Khazvin that in recent years the Believers have constructed a Mashrak-el-Azcar.

One evening at dusk we were conducted thither. Following one of our friends, we were soon lost in the labyrinth of streets of the old part of the city. Going through the ancient bazaars, with their high vaulted roofs, dimly lighted here and there by lanterns, one could easily imagine himself in a great subterranean world. Carefully we picked our way along, fearful of dropping into an open cistern or water-way—quite possible in such places—until we at last descended from the street into the ancient courtyard of the home of Kurratu'l-'Ayn. From here we were taken into the garden, at the farthest end of which stood the Mashrak-el-Azcar. Here, under the portico, many friends were grouped to meet us. Then we entered the building, where the usual entertainment of chanting and a collation was offered us.

Within the precincts of the temple lived a very old believer—one of the original followers of The Bab—who entertained us by recounting many interesting incidents connected with the early days of the movement and with the life of Kurratu'l-'Ayn. On leaving the Mashrak-el-Azcar, we found the garden had been illuminated by lamps, placed about the fountains and along the walks. Passing along an alley of trees and shrubs, which led toward the ancient dwelling, we saw in the distance the veiled figure of a woman standing in the doorway, lights on either side of the portal making her clearly visible in contrast with the surrounding darkness. This was the daughter of our venerable host, the teacher who lived here, and she awaited us with a word of salutation and greeting. As she spoke she parted slightly her chador or veil. We, in turn, gave her the greetings of the maid servants of the Bahai assemblies of the West, asking her to convey the same to the women Bahais of Khazvin. Then, taking leave of the Believers, we ascended to the street and, with the assistance of several friends provided with lanterns, we returned to the house of the hospitable doctor.

In contrast with this meeting in the Mashrak-el-Azcar, I will describe a visit we made the following morning to one of the government prisons. A party of us, after walking through a most beautiful public garden laid off with avenues of stately cypress trees, stopped before some government buildings used to house a garrison. Near by was the city prison and, as we stood, there proceeded from the open doorway a procession of twelve or fifteen prisoners. They were marching in single file, each with a heavy iron collar about his neck, by which he was attached to a long chain which clanked dolefully as the line moved slowly across the court-yard.

When near us the prisoners halted long enough for us to give them some coins for food. They began telling us their various stories. One had been imprisoned for stealing, another for murder, and so it ran. Later on we went into the dungeon, where other prisoners were chained by the neck to a series of irons in the floor, which kept them lying at full length. I go into these painful details to give an idea of a Persian prison, for in these prisons many Bahais have languished and from them gone forth to martyrdom.

Shortly before sunset one evening we set out for Teheran. Several carriages conveyed a party of us to a certain caravanserai, an hour or more

A GROUP OF JEWISH BAHAIS IN TEHERAN.

A BAHAI TRAVELLER

distant from the city, where we all alighted for tea and to bid farewell to one another. One of the friends in Teheran, being notified from Resht of our approach to the capital, had sent a trusted household servant to meet us on the way and render us any possible service. This man joined us in Khazvin, and though we had no special need of him he journeyed onward with us.

It was between twelve and one o'clock that night when we made our first stop at the house of a hitherto unknown friend. We were greeted with the usual hospitality, to which by this time we had become so accustomed that we had almost ceased to wonder at it. It was thought best to remain here for two or three hours for rest before continuing the journey. So, after supper had been served, we were shown to a room where, removing our outer clothing, we laid ourselves down on divans, expecting to get a little sleep.

My friend was remarking that Bahai conditions in Persia were hardly what he had anticipated, for here we were traveling onward to the capital without difficulty, when only a few years previous Bahai blood had flowed in the very places through which we were passing. He had scarcely finished speaking when, from the court-yard below our windows, we heard a murmur of voices which grew in intensity until it became a chorus of loud harangues. Though I knew only a few words of Persian, I understood from these few and from the angry tones, that some people were cursing the Bahai Cause and its adherents and particularly our host, whose voice we could distinguish from time to time expostulating with the crowd. After a few moments he came to our door to express his regret at the occurrence and to assure us that all was well and that there was no prospect of violence. Again, shortly, we heard his voice outside and the din subsided, though for an hour or more there were spasmodic outbursts of rage coming from various directions out of the darkness.

It seems that a company of soldiers was traveling that way and instead of quartering themselves, as was usual, in the caravanserai, which was near, they preferred the shelter of the yard and garden of our friend, where, against his protests, they proceeded to install themselves. At this juncture we arrived, and under the light of the portico of the house they saw him greet us.

Some of the soldiers knew that he was a Bahai, and this fact, together with our hospitable reception, gave sufficient grounds for such a demonstration. Between three and four o'clock in the morning we took our leave. By this time all had quieted down and the agitators, rolled in their blankets, were sleeping on the pavement of the court, while a chorus of snores was all that broke the peace and harmony of the night.

The road from Khazvin to Teheran traverses desolate tracts of arid land, intersected at long intervals by streams, the banks of which are flanked by gardens. In the desert the presence of water gives rise to the most luxuriant vegetation, but when absent, the bleaching bones of beasts of burden strewing the highways, with here and there a great hungry looking vulture, accentuate the contrast between garden and desert and life and death. This same condition we sensed in the soul life of the people whom we met. Entering various Bahai houses along the route, a meal here and a glass of tea there, we were quickened by the kindness and devotion of these friends. They outwardly manifested the life of the indwelling spirit of their faith. On the other hand, we were constantly reminded of the fanaticism and spiritual darkness of the many whom we passed on the highways—men of various religions and castes, who considered us and all, save those of their own cult, as unclean dogs. Surely, if possible, their stare would have killed, but, as it was, it was only painful. There is no fanaticism so intense as that encountered in the Orient.

One of the prophecies relative to this day is that "the desert shall rejoice and blossom as the rose." Indeed we saw the fulfillment of this marvelous verse, for many of the people who were kindest to us had, only a comparatively short time before, been as desert land untouched by the spirit. Of one man, particularly kind to us, we asked how long he had been a Bahai, thinking that he had acquired his illumination through years of service. To our question he replied: "Thirty-one days," speaking as if it had been a lifetime in itself and, verily, so it had, for he had been born again. As in the desert the presence of water gives rise to most luxuriant vegetation, so it is in the desert of men's souls, when the life-giving water of the spirit of God enters it gives rise to the fruits of the kingdom.

A BAHAI TRAVELLER 93

While crossing a parched plain four or five hours from Teheran, our carriage broke down. After some little difficulty the damage was sufficiently repaired to allow us to proceed at a moderate pace for a mile or more, until we arrived at a post-khaneh kept by a friend, who, when we explained that we would be obliged to remain there for several hours for repairs, quite frankly showed his delight at the prospect of a visit. This man was from Esphahan, where our people have suffered much at the hands of the fanatical Moslems, as well as by the oppression of unscrupulous rulers.

In speaking of the Bahais in Persia, and their relations with those in the West, this believer struck the keynote when he said that in his country the Bahais had suffered such long and strenuous persecution and trouble, that they had become tired and heartsick, and needed the association and moral support of the friends of the West. How often we thought of the reverse conditions existing in the West, where we are in need of this spirit, which the Oriental Bahais have received through suffering. The West needs what the East has to give and the East needs what the West has to give it. This interchange can take place only as the two come together in love and harmony. In the past Occidentals have gone to the Orient and Orientals to the Occident, but because of an absence of basic unity—religious unity—no lasting good has come to either. Now how different is this when, in the Bahai Cause, Easterners go West and Westerners go East, meeting on the common ground of faith, for then each returns to his own country and people refreshed in soul and buoyant with a force and knowledge which help him to face his problems and demonstrate to him the conquering power of spiritual oneness, the mission of the Bahai Cause.

Taking leave of this friend from Esphahan, we proceeded eastward toward Teheran. About two hours before sunset we sighted the domes and minarets of the capital, rich in color, rising from the floor of the plain against a background of the snow-clad Elburz. As we neared the city we saw ahead several carriages driving rapidly toward us. These were at first distinguishable only by the clouds of dust which enveloped them. Then, as they drew quite near to us, we distinguished the occupants eagerly looking out ahead. Instinctively we knew these to be friends, and, almost before the drivers could rein in the horses they had descended and surrounded our carriage.

After an affectionate welcome, we found ourselves laden with flowers which these friends had brought to us. To the traveler of the desert nothing is more refreshing than to bury his face in fragrant flowers. After traveling for hours in clouds of dust under a parching sun, without a vestige of vegetation, he really appreciates vegetable life and the fragrance of the flowers when finally he finds himself within the enclosure of a garden. So it is with us, spiritually, we meet souls who are alive in the Lord; their presence is an oasis in the desert of the world and contact with them is soul refreshing and invigorating. Thus we found the flowers, brought us, symbolic of the spiritual aspect of our meeting with the Teheran friends.

Before reaching the city gates, we halted before the entrance of a large and beautiful garden, where we were met by more friends. Entering the garden and passing along beside waterways and avenues of trees and shrubs, we came to an open summer pavilion, where tea and other refreshments were served us.

After the sacred chants, which characterize all reunions of our people in the East, we conversed for a time, delivering messages and letters brought with us from friends in other places, as well as giving accounts of the work in the West. Shortly before sunset the party entered the city, several of the friends accompanying us to the quarters where it had been arranged that we should be installed.

As I have already stated, just before our entering on Persian soil, there had been revolution and bloodshed in Teheran. By the time, however, that we reached the capital all was tranquil. Had it not been for the ruins and the debris of the buildings, lately cannonaded, there would have been no visible traces of the recent troubles. In fact, we found the Bahais there in the utmost peace and happiness. As they had taken no part in the political troubles of the day they were in the good esteem and respect of the government, and now were enjoying unusual privileges. On account of the revolution no gatherings of any nature were allowed by the police, yet upon several occasions the Bahais ob-

A BAHAI TRAVELLER

tained permission to hold meetings numbering as many as four hundred and more souls. Several of the Bahais had been appointed to high governmental positions and a general spirit of assurance and safety characterized the assembly, which was quite different from anything hitherto known there in the history of the cause. Now many of the friends in Teheran are known as Bahais and it does not seem to embarrass them, whereas not many years ago it would have meant death. This freedom in the capital bespeaks rapid progress in the cause throughout the country in the near future, because, being the life and center of all things in Persia, the influence of Teheran is widely felt throughout the various cities and provinces.

I will not attempt to give a detailed description of the series of breakfasts, excursions, receptions and dinners which we attended in Teheran, but I will make mention of a few meetings and entertainments which were typical of the many accorded us. Fortunately a most tranquil spirit of repose characterizes Bahai entertainments in the East, otherwise we had not been able to keep up the round as we did, day and night, from week to week. While the spiritual feature of all meetings was the more important, nevertheless one's material wants were never disregarded, and every possible thing was done for our bodily comfort. The social events of the day usually began at sunrise when tea was served, after which visits were usually received until nine or ten o'clock, when we would start forth to the house where we happened to be lunching that day, or on some excursion about the city. Lunch was usually served at noon and was followed by a nap, from which we would be aroused for tea before going to a late afternoon gathering of Believers, invariably held in some garden—few if any houses being large enough to accommodate these large afternoon reunions. The evenings were always spent at the house of some friend where we dined, the dinner being served about ten o'clock.

During my stay in Teheran, because of poltical agitations, there was fear of an uprising of the people, so no one was allowed to circulate in the streets after eleven o'clock at night without a special permit. Several times we had this permission through the kind efforts of friends, but on various other occasions we spent the night at the house where we dined, sleeping usually out of doors as is the summer custom of the Persians.

At the home of one of the friends of the cause there was a subterranean bath built for the most part below the level of a garden. This was placed at our disposal during our sojourn there. A flight of steps led from the ground level down to the vaulted chambers of the bath, which were floored with slabs of marble, while the walls, up to a certain height, were set with rare old tiles. The bath in the East is quite a lengthy process with its hot and cold water douches and massaging, and it is invariably followed by refreshments, conversation and a nap. After bathing here the morning following our arrival in Teheran, we went into a neighboring garden, where a number of our friends awaited us, and where we were refreshed with sherbet.

One of our good brothers, an Israelite just graduated in medicine, was delegated by the assembly to serve us as guide, to make out a schedule of meetings and entertainments, and to see that we arrived at the appointed places at the scheduled times. I will never cease to marvel at the devotion and unselfish service of this young man. He was with us practically all the time doing everything in his power to make things as agreeable and as comfortable as possible. Had I traveled to Teheran to meet him only, I should have considered my time well spent and a valuable lesson learned. Lessons in brotherly devotion one can see exemplified in the lives of these eastern brothers, for they have suffered for the cause until friendship and devotion have become dominant characteristics.

Among the many who entertained us were two young men, sons of the noted Bahai teacher and poet, Vargha who, together with another son of but twelve years, Ruollah, suffered a martyr's death during one of the later persecutions in Teheran. For several years the bodies of these martyrs lay in a common grave, where they had been flung by their executioners. After matters had become more tranquil for the Bahais their remains were removed in the night and with the greatest difficulty, and given a befitting entombment.

When we were told of this matter, we asked that we might visit the tomb of these two martyrs. Consequently, the following morning the younger son came and escorted us thither. In the center of a beautiful garden, at some little

A BAHAI TRAVELLER 101

distance from the city, stood the mausoleum. It consisted of a nine-sided chamber, about twenty-five feet in diameter, enclosed by massive walls. Beneath the floor were the two tombs. The building was surrounded by a portico and colonnade. Three flights of steps ascended from the ground to the floor of the portico, while three doors gave access to the interior. Nine avenues diverged from the building to various parts of the garden, while canals of water intersected it in various directions.

Entering the mausoleum, our friend chanted a tablet and prayer written by Abdul-Baha specially to be read when the Bahais gather here. The chanting over, we remained for a few moments in silent prayer before withdrawing to the garden. I wish I might adequately describe the impression produced by the visit to this shrine. We were in a way brought closer than before to the sufferings and heroic sacrifices of the Persian Bahais, through which the holy cause grew and expanded until now it encircles the earth. We in the West little realize the debt of gratitude we owe to the East for the holy teaching which now is given to us so freely, and which we accept while seated at our ease, for it came to us only after it had attained its growth in the Orient under the fire of the most savage persecution.

The spirit of the friends who suffered so in Persia is indeed inspiration and food for the soul. During the return drive to the city, our young friend spoke of the martyrdom of his father and brother and told us that often as he walked the streets he passed the man who killed them, yet, so happy is he that they were permitted to serve the religion by dying for it, and so strong in his own faith, there is no room left in his soul for harboring enmity for those through whom his troubles came.

I mention this one specific case, which was but one of many. On all sides we heard of the troubles and persecutions of our people, but not once did we hear so much as a suggestion of anything which savored of antagonism or hatred toward the persecutors. This and the unity and solidarity of the Persian Bahais impressed me more than all else in Persia. The strength of a chain is measured by the strength of its individual links. And this is likewise true in the assembly of Believers. The work accomplished by the body is in proportion to the strength and steadfastness of its individual members.

Since returning to America, many people have asked me about the condition of Bahai women in Persia. Compared with our acquaintance with men, our acquaintance with the women was but slight; nevertheless, from seeing even a few women and by talking with many men upon the subject, we were able to form at least an idea of existing conditions.

In Persia, as in most Oriental countries, the conventions of society demand the seclusion of women. Through the influence of the Bahai teachings, we found our people to be quite rid of that mental attitude so generally held in the Orient—that woman is in every way man's inferior and should be his slave. The Bahais in Persia are doing all in their power for the education and training of women. In a recent tablet from Abdul-Baha, regarding education, he writes of the necessity of the education of boys and then goes on to demonstrate how much more necessary it is that girls should be educated and trained, because they—the girls—are to be the mothers and the educators and trainers of the coming generation. The attitude of the Bahais in Persia toward women is quite that held by most enlightened people in the West, but on account of existing social conditions and the persecution of our people, they are not yet able to carry out their ideas and aspirations.

Even after visiting Persia it is almost impossible to comprehend the hatred of the people toward the Bahais. Fanatical by nature and creed-bound, the Moslem hates everything outside of his own realm of thought, and when he sees his own people adopting new ideas his wrath is often uncontrollable and he goes forth to kill. By this reign of ignorance some of the difficulties under which the Bahai reformers are working can be imagined. In the early days of the movement, with all the enthusiasm of newly awakened souls, the Believers sought with fervor to bring about quick changes in Persia. They taught unguardedly and raised so much antagonism that the cause was all but exterminated by the massacres which ensued. Such troubles characterized the days of The First Point— The Bab—and also the beginning of the ministry of Baha'o'llah. However, under the guidance of the latter the Bahais learned to be cautious and careful in their religious work until

A BAHAI TRAVELLER

now, avoiding disagreement and friction with the opposers, they are peacefully and steadily working and changing ignorance into knowledge and hatred into love.

Under these improving conditions the women are naturally becoming more and more, as we term it in the West, "emancipated." The work is difficult and slow, but it is being accomplished, and here is an open door to us Bahais of the West, a practical way of service, for through our co-operation our brothers and sisters in the East will be helped and encouraged, and through unity with us they will learn many things. On the other hand, we will ourselves receive more abundantly than we give. The East has much to give to the West, as well as the West has much to give to the East. This interchange will take place as the two come together in spiritual unity and in practical service one to the other.

In Persia one meets people who, after long or brief sojourns in western Europe, have accumulated certain western ideas, which they have mingled with those of Persian origin, producing a mixture neither one thing nor the other, occidental nor oriental—ideas which are not applicable to conditions in Persia, because they are the products of a foreign civilization evolved under foreign conditions.

One of the most interesting characters we met in Persia was a certain khanum (lady) of Teheran, a woman of ability as a leader of women. For some time past she had been working assiduously for the spread of the Bahai cause among women, and for the education and general uplifting of her sex.

What was most interesting in the working of the Bahai movement in Persia was that it was solving present-day problems in the only practical way, namely, by working from within out—by quickening the soul, from which is begotten the desire for knowledge and its accompanying advantages.

This was exemplified in the work of the khanum whom I have mentioned. She was an enlightened soul, holding advanced ideas, not gleaned from foreign sources, but evolved through personal work and service. She was wholly a product of Persia and was, therefore, able to understand and to minister unto the needs of those among whom she labored.

I must describe a meeting which we attended at the house of the khanum mentioned, since it gave us a glimpse of oriental life and conditions hitherto not seen. Our hostess had for some time past discarded her veil and with her husband received men in her house and garden, yet she was obliged, as she explained to us, to veil in the streets on acount of attracting too much attention. On this particular afternoon she was holding two receptions at once. Twenty or more of us men were in one room, while in an adjoining room, separated from us by a curtain, was a party of twelve or fifteen ladies, our hostess slipping quietly from one room to the other, serving and entertaining her guests.

After the chanting of tablets, my companion and I were asked to tell the ladies in the next room something about their sisters in the West, which we did to the best of our ability, he speaking in Persian while my words were translated and spoken through the curtain to the listeners on the other side. Our hostess, it seemed, had hoped that the women in the next room would on that day follow her example and unveil. As we spoke of the freedom and independence and higher education of woman in the West, the khanum became more and more enthusiastic until, finally, she went toward the doorway and drawing the curtain began speaking very earnestly to the people in the next room. I could not understand her words but so stirring was the tone of her voice that I caught the spirit of what she was saying. She was calling to her sisters to come forth and lift their veils, saying that it was a rare opportunity to do so then, since we from the West were there, who were accustomed to seeing women's faces. At the expiration of several minutes her words had the desired effect, for the women arose and drawing aside their veils with one accord, entered the room.

The men made place for the ladies by retreating to the other side of the room, while the newcomers found seats. When the women had arisen to the situation, they were quite equal to it. Curious as this may seem to one accustomed to western conventionalities, it showed that these women were awake to the advantages of the western women as well as to their own disadvantage. I was particularly impressed by the possibilities for work among the women of Persia by the Bahai women of the West. The eagerness with which these women listened to our account of western life in itself showed that the time was ripe and that they were anxious and waiting to be taught.

As we were leaving the house, the khanum took from her neck an interesting necklace of mother of pearl and silver, a gift to her from a princess of the royal household, and handed it to me, saying that it was for the Bahai women in America, and with it went the love and greeting of the Bahai maid-servants in Teheran. On my return to America, I entrusted this souvenir to the care of Mrs. Isabella D. Brittingham, who has already organized a system of correspondence between some of the meetings of Bahai women in America with gatherings of women in various cities in Persia. This is but the beginning of a great work for the women of our western assemblies to do among their sisters of the East. Through correspondence the way will be opened for western women to go to those distant parts as teachers, nurses, physicians, and what they will be able to accomplish cannot be estimated.

One very interesting morning was spent in visiting one of the leading boys' schools in Teheran. On account of the attitude of the Moslems, this institution is not known generally as a Bahai school. However, it is in reality in the hands of the Bahais. From the directors down through the teachers and students the majority were of our faith. We were taken around through the various class rooms, where over two hundred boys were engaged in reciting and study. Before starting on our travels, my friend had planned to remain for some time in Teheran, so he was very much pleased when told that they needed a teacher of English in this school and he was glad to undertake the work. Shortly after I left Teheran, his duties as teacher there commenced. I understand that in other parts of Persia teachers of English are needed among the Bahais. Undoubtedly, in the near future, the way will be open for Bahais from the West to go to the East to fill these positions. This is a good field for work in the cause, since the people there are greatly helped and strengthened by intercourse with the western Bahais.

One Saturday afternoon, about an hour before sunset, we were conducted through the bazaars to the Jewish quarter to the house of a certain doctor, where a hundred and more of Israelitish Bahais were gathered to welcome us. During the walk thither, we passed a place of Bahai interest, namely, the house where Abdul-Baha was born on May 23, 1844, the same day upon which The Bab declared Himself. At the end of a street one can see a small second-story arcade, behind which is the room in which our great teacher first saw the light of this world. This house was not open to us, so we gazed upon it from without for a few moments and then passed on.

Although there are no lines of distinction whatever between the Bahais, yet, in places where persecution exists, those previously of a like faith meet together, not wishing to attract too much attention. In Teheran there are between twenty and thirty weekly meetings held in various quarters of the city, so that all may easily participate. The Jewish meeting which I mention was composed chiefly of Jewish Believers, but there were also present Christians, Moslems and Zoroastrians. In Persia there is a type of Jew which we in the West seldom see. There the Jews have lived in their communities for centuries, and consequently have kept their original type and spirit less changed than those who have lived for generations wandering amongst the various nations of the world. Like their orthodox brethren in the West, the Jews in Persia have retained their ancient faith in the fulfillment of the prophecies of their scriptures, and they look for the Messiah and the regeneration of the whole world. This has made them particularly open to the Bahai Message, and in places there are whole communities of them who have accepted the faith. Hamadan is the chief center of Jewish Bahais in Persia. Here they have their own schools and are carrying on other active and progressive works.

At the Jewish meeting I mentioned, several of the older men in long robes and turbans spoke, welcoming us and expressing their joy at uniting spiritually with us in accepting Baha-'o'llah as the promised latter-day Messiah, through whose teaching they now accept the Christ whom their forefathers rejected. This meeting was one of the most memorable of our travels. The reunion over, a dinner was served, after which we mounted to a terraced roof. Here mats, rugs, cushions and bedding had been spread, and it was not long before each had made himself comfortable for the night. I lay awake for some time looking up at the stars and think-

A BAHAI TRAVELLER 113

ing of the significance of that evening's gathering. This was the beginning of the time when all peoples, Jew and Gentile, will be united in His kingdom.

The first large meeting of Bahais which we attended in Teheran was a Zoroastrain or Parsee reunion. This was held in a garden belonging to a friend of the cause—a garden which was the most beautiful I visited while in Persia, having artificial lakes, surrounded and separated by forest trees, vistas extending off toward the north, affording views of the distant mountains highest of which towered Mount Damovend with its mantle of snow and ice. A series of avenues and walks flanked by water-ways and flower beds, formed a beautiful setting for the two palaces and several pavilions which were in the midst of the garden. The place of meeting was under the broad portico of the smaller of the two palaces, which was originally built by the unfortunate Atabok-Azam (who died by the assassin's hand), Prime Minister to the late Mozaffer-Ed-Din-Shah. The pavement of the portico was carpeted and chairs were placed about for some of the guests, others sitting down Persian fashion on the rugs. One of the features of the meeting was the chanting of an original poem of welcome to us, which was written by one of the friends—the whole assembly joining in the refrain. Several of the friends present spoke to us regarding the Zoroastrain prophecies which were fulfilled in the coming of The Bab and Baha'o'llah, and explained that in the Zoroastrian teaching the final unity of all people was taught and that now the Zoroastrians were accepting the Bahai teaching as that which their people had long hoped to realize—the uniting of all men in the brotherhood of the kingdom

---

On another like occasion, in the afternoon, we met in another garden, where a large number of Moslem Bahais were gathered to greet us. Because of the crowd all could not be accommodated in any one place, so they were grouped in various parts of the garden thus forming several centers. As the twilight fell, lamps were placed about the fountains and along the walks, and then the chanting began. We sat near a basin of water about which were grouped many men, soldiers from the Shah's cossaque guard, in their red uniforms, while their officers wore blue, together with men wearing robes of many and varied colors. These and the lights with their reflection in the water, the natural beauty of the place, the distant strains of chanting which reached our ears alternately from the various groups of friends scattered throughout the garden, made an impression which will long remain with me.

Here among the Moslem Bahais we heard the same story of how they believed because of their own prophecies which foretold the coming of the Lord in these latter days and the establishment of His kingdom. In many ways they expressed their joy and satisfaction at having us with them. One remarked to me that more of the joy of the kingdom was realized when those of different faiths were brought together in this cause, than by the uniting of those who had previously held the same faith. In the East, where the devotees of the various religions hate one another so cordially, the contrast is indeed striking when we see them uniting in the Bahai cause and fraternizing as members of one family.

One of the friends who entertained us, a Jewish doctor, together with another Jewish physician, is running a dispensary and hospital in Teheran. One morning we went there for a visit. A cheerful court-yard with its fountain and flowers from which opened the various rooms of the building with their accommodation for twenty-eight patients, formed the necessary elements of a hospital—an institution of which Persia is much in need. Comparing this hospital with ours in the West, it seemed very primitive but, considering the conditions of the country it was far, far beyond the local standard of hygiene in its appointments. These friends are laboring under great difficulties, as do all those who try to lift the masses of inert humanity in the East. Nevertheless, their work is gaining in proportion and in momentum. They, too, need the helping hand of the western friends. A Bahai woman physician working with them could accomplish much, both of a spiritual as well as a physical nature. She could reach the women and the inner life of the people by ways not open in the East to men of the profession, and through service and example her influence as an educator would be far-reaching.

After the work of ministering to the health of the people in Persia, the most important thing to be undertaken is the teaching of industries.

HADJEE AMEEN AND HADJEE AKHOUNT
TWO BAHAIS IMPRISONED FOR THEIR FAITH.

A BAHAI TRAVELLER

There is a great field for industrial work in all parts of that country. Persia is rich in mineral deposits and in other natural resources. These must be developed, and for the best good of all must be developed by the people themselves. That they might do so they must first be taught. Now the sons of the wealthy go from Persia to the various capitals of Europe for educational purposes, but that is not practical nor sufficient. It is necessary that special and advanced education be placed within the reach of the mass of the people. To the young brought up in the simplicity of Oriental surroundings life in a European metropolis is filled with temptations which he is not prepared to withstand. Thus many, after years of schooling abroad, lose their natural charm and simplicity, without having acquired the real virtues of the West. They fall away from their own country and people and at the same time are not fitted for life in western countries.

The salvation of Persia must—like that of all peoples—he worked out from within. She has great possibilities, and through the practical education of her sons and daughters she will lift herself to her ancient prosperity and place among the great nations of the world. Now her vital moral forces are spent, corruption, oppression and laxity of morals hold despotic sway over her people, keeping them down to the earth. Her predominating religion, that of Islam, once so powerful a factor for the betterment of the Orient, has lost its power as a religion and nothing of it remains save creed, dogma and fanaticism. The only thing which can rejuvenate Persia and save her is a spiritual uplift that shall quicken the soul of her people and infuse into them that force needed to redeem it.

In Persia the Bahais are laying the foundation of this great national uplift, but they are now at a point where they need the co-operation of the Bahais of the West. The more we in the West correspond with our brothers in the Orient, the more we go there to travel and to live and work among them, the more we will be helping them in their great task of bettering humanity.

At last the day appointed for me to take leave of my American brother and the other friends arrived. I was loath to turn westward, but my vacation was limited and, as Abdul-Baha, in

Akka had asked me to return to see him on my way home I felt I must be off. At an early hour I was taken with my luggage to the garden without the city, where we had been entertained on the day of our arrival. Here the day was spent in one continuous reception, for almost every one of the hundreds we had met in Teheran joined the gathering at some time during the protracted festivities. At noon we all walked to one end of the garden, where the ground was covered with mats and rugs upon which were spread in Persian fashion cloths laden with food and flowers. Sitting about on the ground we lunched, after which we had a nap under the shelter of a summer house, followed by tea and more feasting. Shortly before dusk we parted with all save about twenty of our friends, who accompanied us into the city to the near-by house of a Bahai, where we spent the evening in conversation, dining at the usual hour of eleven o'clock.

Mirza Taghi Khan, our constant companion since the Krasnovodsk affair, was now returning to Eshkhabad, which was fortunate for me, for our ways lay together again from Teheran to Baku. A little after midnight our carriage was announced and, with the assistance of many hands, we were soon settled therein with our articles of luggage about us, and after many adieus we left this little group of friends standing in the flickering torchlight looking after us as the carriage rolled away.

A few minutes brought us to the Khazvin gate, where with some difficulty our coachman aroused the sleepy turnkey, who, staggering to his feet, unlocked and opened the ponderous city gates, which, with a rattling of chains and a clanking of bars, closed on us as we drove forth into the night. Another starry night it was, too. Far off in the west hung low upon the horizon a brilliant planet which seemed as a guiding star, indicating, as of old, the direction of the Holy Land.

The down journey from Teheran to Resht was quite the same in character as had been the up journey; we were greeted by the same friends and in the same hospitable way. The drive was broken only at Khazvin, where we spent two days and a night with our friend, the doctor. Hearing of our coming, he met us on the road as before and escorted us into the city. This time we were in open carriages and it not being wise for us to be seen together, we parted just without the city walls, his carriage entering by one gate, ours by another. This time while in Khazvin, I had the opportunity of visiting the Bahai school, in which about fifty young boys were studying under the supervision of instructors. One of these teachers spoke French fluently and he acted as interpreter for me during the visit.

An unbroken ride of thirty-six hours brought us from Khazvin to Resht, where we arrived the middle of the morning. The steamer by which we expected to sail was booked to leave Enzalee at ten thirty that night. After discussing the situation with the friends we decided to drive the twenty-two miles from Resht to Enzalee over a turnpike which traverses the marshes and lowlands separating Resht from the port. The Believers could not comprehend why we should arrive and leave both in the same day and it was with some difficulty that we begged off from remaining three days until the sailing of the next steamer.

Accordingly, after an unavoidable delay, we set out. The further we drove the worse became the road, until, finally, the horses could hardly draw the carriage, the wheels of which were half way up to their hubs in sand and loose earth. Thus so much time was lost that we did not reach Enzalee until the steamer had sailed. The only thing to do was to return to Resht. Leaving at midnight we drove all night, arriving at Resht at daybreak. It was our third night in a carriage, and between the mosquitoes and insects, a drenching fog and mist which rolled in from the sea, and the dismal cries of jackals with which the forests abounded, we had a bad night of it. In Resht, instead of being dismayed at our plight, our friends rejoiced at the prospect of a continued visit, and in the end I was not at all sorry for the experience, for we had three more pleasant days in Persia. On the third day, in good season, three of our friends escorted us to Enzalee and saw us safely on board the steamer for Baku.

On the quay in Baku, we were met by several friends, who had been notified of our coming. Remaining here but a few hours, I parted with my faithful friend and traveling companion, Mirza Taghi Khan, and bidding good-bye to the other friends, traveled westward by rail through Caucasia to Tiflis and to Batum on the Black

Sea. In Batum I spent three very pleasant days with Believers. Here I was joined by a young man from Teheran, whom I had met during my first visit to Khazvin, at which time he was on his way to Resht and Baku. We had hoped to meet at some point along the line of travel between Persia and Akka, since we were both bound for the Holy Land. Boarding a steamer we touched along the ports of Armenia, arriving at Constantinople at the end of four days.

While I was in Persia, the news reached us that a constitutional form of government had been declared in Turkey. Everywhere the Bahais were enthusiastic over this change, for they knew that with the passing of the old regime of despotism, the troubles which had for so many years harassed our leader, Abdul-Baha, would be at an end. On arriving in Constantinople I found great changes taking place. My former visits there had given me a decided dislike for the place. The corruptness of all branches of the government made it impossible to transact any business without bribery. The general corruption of the country was apparent at every turn. This was particularly noticeable in the attitude and bearing of the people. Spied upon, maltreated, and oppressed, they were constrained, fearful, and suspicious. Now, however, all seemed quite different. The people were light-hearted and free, singing songs of liberty and praising the constitution. Newspapers and printed matter, hitherto subject to confiscation, were free to all. There seemed to be an entire change in the very character and soul of the people. During our stay of two days in Constantinople, we met freely with the Oriental Bahais there, they no longer fearing trouble, since the constitution gave the people religious freedom.

From Constantinople, my Persian friend and I took ship for Smyrna, where we made a brief stay, again sailing by a vessel which landed us in Beirut. The nearer we approached Akka the more elated we found our friends. In Syria the changes brought about by the constitution seemed greater than those in Turkey, but probably this was only apparent to us because here we had more vital interests than at the capital. The officials, who had oppressed Abdul-Baha and his people, were no longer in power. Some had fled, barely escaping with their lives; others disappeared, while yet others were in prison.

THE TOMB OF THE BAB UPON MOUNT CARMEL.

The oppressors had been dealt with as they had dealt with others.

The joy of the Bahais was a pleasure to see—especially that of the older men, who had survived years of hardship and oppression in the cause. It was here in Beirut that we first learned of Abdul-Baha's freedom, for, with the going into force of the constitution, all of the political prisoners throughout the realm were liberated, and just before our arrival in the country he had been officially notified of his freedom.

After a visit of four days with the friends in Beirut, we embarked for Haifa. On arrival there, instead of having to await for favorable conditions under which to enter Akka, as had always been necessary in the past, we drove from the quay directly to the house of Abdul-Baha, where we were most graciously received. Although this was not my first visit to Akka, it was the first time that I had seen anything worthy of mention of the city. I went about as a sight-seer. Wearing a tarboosh (fez) and an aba (cloak) with several Oriental friends, I even penetrated into the precincts of the mosque. On another occasion a number of us took a stroll over the plain of Akka, visiting the cemeteries near the city, where are the tombs of Abdul-Baha's mother, brother, and many of the original exiles who came to that country in captivity with Baha'o'llah.

One night I went to the pilgrims' house in Akka, where the Oriental friends are usually entertained. A long walk through dark streets flanked with high buildings, and so narrow they seemed like crevices in the crust of the earth, brought us to an old caravanserai on the side of the city opposite to that where Abdul-Baha lived. In the upper part of this building, with windows and balconies overlooking the sea and Mount Carmel in the distance, are the rooms where the pilgrims are lodged and where several of the Bahai men live. Here we met Hadji Mirza Heyder Ali, a well known Bahai teacher, who spent twelve years in exile for his faith in Khartoum, until freed when the English, under Gordon, entered the city. He is now well along in years and, though feeble in body, is spiritually young and active. When asked about his sufferings in the cause, he was at first not very communicative, but later on he told me some of his experiences.

Abdul-Baha was, as might have been expected,

happy because of the freedom and liberty of the people. As for himself, personally, one did not feel that the change made very much difference one way or another. He seemed removed from the possibility of being hampered by calamity or uplifted by fortune.

Many people have asked me how Abdul-Baha impressed me. I should hardly use the word "impress" in connection with him. An impression is something which is imprinted upon one from without. His influence is not that of one personality upon another. Through contact with him the soul responds, is quickened and refreshed by his spirit of love, humility, service to humanity, and all other kindred virtues. This soul-quickening then produces its regenerating effect upon the character and soul of the individual, working from within outward.

Each time I have gone to Akka I have naturally carried with me a conception or a mental picture of Abdul-Baha, and each time I have been obliged to lay this aside in order to find a larger and higher one. He has remained unchanged, while my vision has been a changing and growing one. Surely, if one were to go to him twenty times, each successive time he would appear different. It is, therefore, better not to cling to preconceived ideas, for unless these all be laid aside the spirit of Baha'o'llah which emanates from him, cannot enter and evolve within us and shape us anew.

Abdul-Baha is a physician, who is healing the spiritual diseases of man. He sees and understands all conditions of the soul and gives to each just what that soul needs. His teaching is simplicity itself. The gospel of love he makes very real through living the life of God's servant among men. His words and explanations are so simple that oftentimes people may at first feel a pang of disappointment, expecting abtruse theories and explanations, but, when they begin to realize the force of the spirit which characterizes Abdul-Baha's life, then they see the real power of his teaching, realizing how much greater is this than philosophizing.

Abdul-Baha teaches that it is through manifesting the joy and giving forth the love of the kingdom that the Bahais will attract hungry souls and be able to lead them to the kingdom. We should be fearless and enthusiastic as he is. We must not think of ourselves nor consider our feelings nor our welfare before that of serving the Lord. We should not be constrained, but should manifest to all, frankly and freely, the love of God which we have in our hearts. The more of this love we give forth, the more of it will be ours to give. There should be no holding back; we must actively serve the Lord in every phase of life, since service is the necessary adjunct of belief and faith, and without works these latter are as naught.

Abdul-Baha's life is essentially one of service. His mission here is to teach us this. Only in following in his path of daily loving service to those about us will we become strong in spirit and fitted to act as stewards of the Lord. We must at all times increase actions, for our words when backed by spiritual actions will not lack force but will produce spiritual results in the souls of those who hear them.

Abdul-Baha sends his greeting and love to the Bahais in the West. In reply to a question regarding the House of Justice,* he said that the House of Justice was not yet established; that for the present there were only local Bahai governing bodies, but that in time we would have a

---
*The teachings of Baha'o'llah provide for the central spiritual body—the House of Justice. Its members will be chosen from the people by the people.

great central convocation composed of members from all parts of the world. This, the House of Justice, will convene at stated times. Its function is administrative; it will, in the spirit of oneness and unity, pass and decide upon matters of moment in the cause, its united action being acceptable before God. Abdul-Baha said that he himself was not under the House of Justice, yet he furthermore said that whatever the Believers agreed upon unanimously he would subscribe to, but this was because of his desire to promote harmony, not that he is subject to the followers.

The day that I left Akka for the West the friends had planned an out-of-door feast in the garden of El-Rizwan, which is not far without the city. After parting with Abdul-Baha and receiving his blessing, in company with an Oriental friend I drove to the tomb of Baha'o'llah, so sacred to His followers, which is at Behji, near Akka. Entering the court of the tomb, we remained for some moments while a tablet was chanted; then, entering the tomb chamber we knelt in silent prayer.

A BAHAI TRAVELLER 131

From Behji we drove to the garden of El-Rizwan, where a large number of the Bahais of the vicinity were assembled. After taking tea and other light refreshments with these friends, seated under the mulberry trees on the terrace beside the river, where Baha'o'llah spent so much time, we had a parting word, a prayer chanted, and many good-byes. Here I left the young man from Teheran who had been my traveling companion for the three weeks past. He had indeed been a friend and typified devotion itself; from him I learned another lesson not taught by word but through example.

Laden with messages of love and greeting to the friends in the West, I started for Haifa, where I arrived just in time to catch an evening steamer for Port Said. From Port Said I went on to Paris, via Messina and Marseilles, where I spent five days with the Believers. Here I met with our well-known friend, M. Ahmed Yazdi, of Port Said, with whom I went to London, in which city we spent five days with the friends before going to Oxford, where Mrs. Stannard and Miss Rosenberg, both of the London assembly, were attending a congress for the comparative study of religion. Miss Rosenberg represented the Bahai Movement at this convocation and read a paper which was well received.

Parting with M. Yazdi, and sailing from Liverpool, I landed in Quebec, and after brief visits with the Bahais in Montreal and New York found myself back again in Washington after an absence of almost six months.

The Persian Bahais have those very elements of spiritual virtue which we in this country need. There is a devotion and a fraternity amongst them which is most beautiful. This is needed in the West. During my trip through the East, I had such a wealth of devotion and brotherly affection poured out upon me that I could actually see and feel its effect. It had refreshed my very soul and quite changed my attitude toward people in general.

This spirit of Bahai love, so intense in Persia, softens and strengthens one's nature. It makes the strong stronger, the weak more firm and steadfast, and it refines man making him more susceptible, and impenetrable to evil. It gives the believer the power to enter into the lives of others and to impart to them the desire to know the truth and the power to arise in service. This is what we all need in greater abundance, is that which Abdul-Baha is giving to us, and it is that which we must attain through following in his path of service to God and mankind.

Finis.

NOTICE.

Copies of this book are sold for sixty cents each; postage paid to any part of the world, ten cents additional.

Address all orders to
>The Bahai Publishing Society.
>>Miss Mary Lesch,
>>>P. O. Box 283,
>>>>Chicago, Ill., U. S. A.

PRICE LIST OF PUBLICATIONS OF THE BAHAI REVELATION.

WORDS OF BAHA'O'LLAH.

The Book of Ighan (Certainty). 190 pages, bound in cloth......$1.00
   Postage 10c additional.
The Tarazet and other Tablets. 92 pages bound in paper......$.50
Surat-ul-Hykl. (The discourse on the Temple.) 63 pages, bound in paper......$.25
The Tablet of Ishrakat. 45 pages, bound in paper......$.25
The Seven Valleys. 56 pages, bound in paper......$.25
Same bound in leather, gilt edges......$1.00
The Hidden Words. 102 pages, bound in paper......$.15
Same bound in leather, gilt edges......$1.00
Lawh-el-Akdas, Kitab-el-Ahd. By Baha'o'llah.
   5c each

ADDRESSES OF ABDUL-BAHA.

Some Answered Questions. By Laura Clifford Barney. 356 pages, bound in cloth......$1.50
   Postage 15c additional.

Tablets of Abdul-Baha—Vol. 1. 238 pages, bound in cloth........................$1.00
    Postage 15c additional.

Abdul-Baha's Addresses in Paris. Bound in paper ....$.75
    Postage 5c additional.

Abdul-Baha's Addresses in London. Bound in paper ....$.40
    Postage 5c additional.

Mysterious Forces of Civilization.........$1.00
    Postage 10c additional.

WRITINGS BY ORIENTAL AND OCCIDENTAL BAHAIS.

Bahai Proofs by Mirza Abul Fazl.........$1.00
    Postage 10c additional.

The Brilliant Proof. By Mirza Abul Fazl Gulpaygan. Bound in paper................$.15

The Universal Religion. By M. Hippolyte Dreyfus. 175 pages, bound in paper....$1.00
    Postage 10c additional.

The Bahai Revelation. By Thornton Chase. 187 pages, bound in paper..............$.50
    Postage 10c additional.

In Galilee. By Thornton Chase. 84 pages, bound in paper, illustrated..............$.25

The Bahai Movement. By Chas. Mason Remey. Bound in cloth........................$.50
    Postage 10c additional.

Observations of a Bahai Traveler. By Chas. Mason Remey. Illustrated and bound in cloth ....$.60
    Postage 10c additional.

Dawn of Knowledge and the Most Great Peace. By Paul Kingston Dealy. 48 pages, bound in paper ....$.15

The Revelation of Baha'o'llah. By Mrs. Isabella D. Brittingham. 32 pages, bound in paper ....$.10

Martyrdom in Persia in 1903. By Hadji Mirza Hayder Ali. 12 pages, bound in paper....$.10

The Oriental Rose. By Mary Hanford Ford. Bound in cloth........................$.60

Ten Days in the Light of Acca. By Mrs. Julia M. Grundy. 111 pages, bound in paper..$.25

Daily Lessons Received at Acca. By Mrs. Goodall and Mrs. Cooper. 80 pages, bound in paper ....$.20

My Visit to Abbas Effendi (Abdul-Baha) in 1899. By Mrs. Margaret B. Peeke. Bound in paper ....$.15

Unity Through Love. By Howard MacNutt. 32 pages, bound in paper..............$.10
Table Talks with Abdul-Baha. By Mr. and Mrs. George T. Winterburn. 32 pages, bound in paper ....$.10
My Visit to Acca. By Mrs. Mary L. Lucas. 42 pages, bound in paper.................$.10
Flowers from the Rose Garden of Acca. By Mrs. Finch and Misses Knobloch. 40 pages, bound in paper......................$.10

MISCELLANEOUS.

Portfolio of Views of The Holy Land. 18 colored sheets, heavy paper cover........$1.00
With portrait of Abdul-Baha, cloth cover. $1.25
Songs of Prayer and Praise. Strongly bound,
$.10

Distributed by the
BAHAI PUBLISHING SOCIETY.
Address all orders to
Miss Mary Lesch,
P. O. Box 283,
Chicago, Ill., U. S. A.

www.ingramcontent.com/pod-product-compliance
Lightning Source LLC
Chambersburg PA
CBHW061325040426
42444CB00011B/2782